DEFENSING THE DELAWARE WING-T

Bob Kenig

Harding Press
Haworth, New Jersey

Library of Congress Cataloging-in-Publication Data

Kenig, Bob
    Defensing the Delaware Wing-T / Bob Kenig.
        p.   cm.
    ISBN 0-9624779-0-7
    1. Football--Defense.   I. Title.   II. Title: Delaware Wing-T.
GV951.18.K45   1990
796.332'2--dc20   89-48397
                                                                    CIP

ISBN 0-9624779-0-7

Printed in the United States of America

HARDING PRESS
P.O. Box 141
Haworth, NJ 07641

Books by and for the coaching profession

MY DAD

As a young man he was not a great scholar,
  but he was an exceptional athlete.
He participated in football, boxing, basketball
  and even the Penn Relays Meet.
He was short and slim, quick and tough.
  To this day he will not turn his back on a fight,
  but he was sweet and kind and gentle enough
  to pick my Mom and together they are just right.
In the football season of my sophomore year
  I told him I wanted to "pack it in."
He told me something that I've heard again and again.
  "Winners never quit and quitters never win."
If I missed a block or tackle during a Saturday game,
  When I got home he would say, "It's your
  fault, son. The Coach is not to blame."
We would talk about football at dinner every autumn night.
  No matter how much I complained about not
  playing or being criticized, to him,
  The Coach was always right.
Even today if I have a problem, no matter what the cause,
  I go to him for advice without a moment's pause.
You all know my Dad. Every game, he is the first one in the stands.
  He says a little prayer that we win,
  with the program clenched firmly in his hands.
Now in the autumn of his years, we grow closer every day.
  My only hope is that when he looks on the
  field tonight, he thinks, "God, I'm proud
  of that boy in every possible way."

by Bob Kenig

Foreword

I have had the pleasure of coaching with Bob Kenig for five years and sharing football information with him for even more years.

He is a dedicated, hard-working and knowledgeable football coach. He utilized the Delaware Wing-T offense during his head coaching career and also defended the same many times during this same tenure. During his career at Widener University, he has also been involved with defending this same potent offense. Our own offense utilizes many of the facets of the Wing-T, and we constantly discuss the Delaware principles from our view from both sides of the ball.

In addition, during his career Coach Kenig has researched many of the experts for their defensive ideas as to how to stop the Wing-T. The end result is his well-done treatise on the subject. Consequently, Bob Kenig, very qualified to write this dissertation on defending the Wing-T, has presented many excellent ideas which I am sure will help you in preparing your defensive game plans for halting the Delaware Wing-T.

Bill Manlove
Head Football Coach/Athletic Director
Widener University

How This Book Will Help You

The Wing-T Offense is the most dynamic offensive system in football today. The formation multiplicity, various uses of motion, pre-snap changes of strength, misdirection running attack and run-oriented passing game have caused many problems for defensive coaches on all levels of competition. The 3-4 "Slant" and "Read Blitz" present a new and successful method of coping with and stopping this potent offensive package.

My fascination with the Wing-T began as a high school head coach in 1975. After little success defending against the Wing-T and a very poor record of 3-8, we embarked upon an extensive study of the offense. We frequently met with offensive staff members from the University of Delaware, home of the Wing-T, and Lehigh University, who also used the offense at the time. We talked with many high school coaches, who were having success running the Wing-T, and spent countless hours viewing high school and college films. We did everything possible to learn and fully understand this innovative system.

As a result of all we learned, and our desire to abandon our 4-3 reading defense, we developed an attacking eight-man-front defense. This defensive scheme made use of a three-deep secondary and used a slanting front as its main mode of attack. This defense was the subject of my first book, *Football's Attacking Combination-60 Defense*. The new defense, coupled with our newly installed Wing-T offense, led us to a school record 10-1 season, a league championship, and the number-five ranking in Pennsylvania. However, as offenses began to increase their passing attacks and spread the defense with multiple wide receivers, we realized modifications had to be made to cope with these new problems.

In 1987, my first season back at Widener University, we employed a multiple seven-man-front defense, allowing the flexibility of four secondary defenders to help handle the ever-increasing passing game and open formations. Against our first Wing-T opponent, we allowed sixty-six running plays for a very unacceptable 211 yards. This run-oriented, ball-control offense achieved its goal of keeping our powerful offense off the field, while giving us our first loss of the young season.

After that game, we analyzed our use of a multiple seven front and settled on a 3-4 as our basic defensive set. We made the Slant and Read Blitz an integral part of our package, especially against Wing-T opponents. During the remainder of that season, and in 1988, we faced eight opponents who employed the Wing-T or some variation of it. Those opponents averaged seventy-one yards rushing per game on forty-one attempts. We also intercepted thirteen passes and recovered fourteen fumbles. The 3-4 Slant and Read Blitz solved the Wing-T dilemma. We stopped the Wing-T running game and had enough secondary support against the run, while sufficiently defending against the spread formations and increased passing game.

For those coaches who are seeking a new and innovative method of attacking the Wing-T Offense, the 3-4 Slant and Read Blitz present a highly successful approach. The fronts, while being simple to teach and equally uncomplicated to learn, present major blocking problems for the offense. These blocking problems hinder the execution of both the running and passing games. The use of both the zone, with the Slant, and a combination zone and man-to-man coverage, with the Read Blitz, keeps the passing game off balance. The constant disguising of the secondary coverages further complicates the problems faced by the quarterback wishing to pass. Correct pre-snap secondary reads are nearly impossible.

When the Slant is used, an inside or outside linebacker executes a blitz. The direction of the Slant determines which linebacker will stunt. The Read Blitz allows as many as all four linebackers to fire on a play. The outside linebackers blitz on all passing plays. The actions of the offensive guards determine how and when the inside linebackers execute a stunt. These linebacker games cause additional confusion and, while forcing the offense off schedule, cause many costly offensive errors.

This book contains all aspects of defending against the Wing-T Offense with the 3-4 Slant and Read Blitz. The many strengths and few weaknesses of the Wing-T attack are thoroughly analyzed. All aspects of installing the Slant and Read Blitz are covered in detail. The actual application of the Slant and Read Blitz against the basic Wing-T plays is explained and diagrammed. Defending against the Sweep, Trap, FB Belly, HB Counter, Belly Option, Sprint Option, Waggle Pass, Play-Action Passes, and Sprint-Out Passes, from many formations is totally broken down. Finally, alignment adjustments to many of the more complex Wing-T variations are clearly discussed.

Adopting all, or part, of the defensive concepts in this book will greatly enhance any coach's ability to deal with and stop the Wing-T Offense. However, there is a very important point to remember: When discussing these ideas with a Wing-T offensive coach, the coach who has the chalk last, WINS!

Contents

Chapter 1

Understanding the Strengths and Weaknesses of the Wing-T Offense

An understanding of the strengths and weaknesses of the Wing-T Offense is critical for the coach who wishes to defend against it. Those coaches who have had success stopping the offense have taken the time to learn a great deal about it. This learning experience is required when defending against any offense and is especially true versus the intricacies of the Wing-T.

STRENGTHS

Basic Backfield Alignment

An analysis of two of the most basic Wing-T sets reveals the problems caused by the placements of the halfbacks and fullback. (Diagrams 1-1, 1-2) The halfbacks align in three positions; these are wing, slot, and setback.

Alignment as a wing creates an additional gap along the line of scrimmage and presents the defense with the immediate threat of three quick receivers: the wing, the tight end, and the split end. The nearness of the wing to the tight end can create switching problems for a man-to-man secondary coverage when they run crossing patterns.

DIAGRAM 1-1

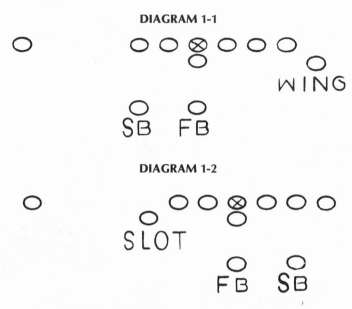

DIAGRAM 1-2

Alignment as a slot, in essence, establishes a double tight-end formation and gives the offense the ability to run off-tackle to both sides. The slot alignment also forces the defense to deal with three quick receivers: the tight end, slot, and split end.

When aligned as a wing or slot, the halfback is in a position to be a blocker or a pass receiver. However, without the use of short motion to place him in a setback position, his availability as a ballcarrier is limited.

When aligned as a setback, the halfback is in his most flexible position. From this alignment, behind the offensive tackle, he is able to execute the same blocks and run the same pass patterns as a wing or slot. Unlike his two other alignments, he is in an excellent position to become an effective ballcarrier.

The alignment of the fullback provides the offense with a balanced attack to either side of the ball. To either side of the formation, the fullback can block for the quarterback on Sprint Action, run the Dive or be a lead blocker. From this middle alignment, he is able to be an effective part of the Wing-T misdirection running attack and is capable of becoming the third receiver to either side.

Multiplicity of Formation

When preparing to defend against most offensive schemes, it is assumed the offense will employ formations with a primary backfield set of one, two, or three running backs. Variations in formations do occur, but variations as to the number of backs in the backfield are much less common. The Wishbone uses a three-back set but will break the Bone and go to a one- or two-back set. The Pro Offense uses two backs but may go to a single-back set in order to get four quick receivers on or near the line of scrimmage. The Run and Shoot Offense employs a single-back set but may motion a slot, wing, or flanker into the backfield to get a two-running-back formation.

The Wing-T Offense is quite unique. It employs, in reality, a three-running-back set. However, during any game, a one-, two- or three-running-back set may be used with equal frequency. Unlike many offenses, the three Wing-T backs are expected to have the same proficiency at blocking, receiving, and rushing. The versatility of the backs gives the offense the flexibility to use, not only multiple backfield sets, but multiple formations.

Multiple backfield sets and numerous pre-movement formations are not the only problems the defensive coach must consider. The offense also employs pre-snap formation changes. These changes occur through the use of various shifts and motions. These pre-snap movements are used to confuse the opponent, get an offensive advantage, and cause defensive errors. Proponents of the Wing-T hope these movements will allow the offense to outflank the defense and give the offense a numerical advantage at the point of attack. The possibility of pre-snap shifts and motions has the tendency of keeping the defense slightly off-balance, while awaiting some kind of formation change. This problem can make the defense susceptible to plays run on a quick count.

Pre-snap shifts are an integral part of the Wing-T Offense and many different ones are employed. Perhaps the most significant shifts are those that change the strength of the offense. These present particular problems for those defensive teams who employ weakside and strongside personnel. One purpose for shifting strength is to cause a dilemma for this type of defense. The defensive coach must decide to shift his personnel with the change of strength or play them out of position. (Diagram 1-3)

DIAGRAM 1-3

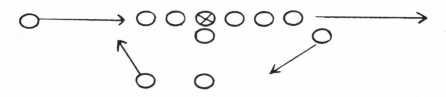

The other type of pre-snap movement is the use of motion. The Wing-T uses three different types of motion: two-step motion, short motion, and extended motion.

Two-step motion occurs when the set halfback motions toward the ball. On the snap of the ball, he is approximately where the tailback is in an I-formation. This motion is used as part of the Belly Series and only slightly changes the offensive formation. However, it puts the halfback in a much better position to be a pitch man on the Option play or a blocker on a Play-Action Pass. (Diagrams 1-4, 1-5)

DIAGRAM 1-4

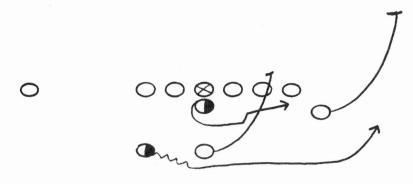

DIAGRAM 1-5

When the slot or wing motions to a setback alignment, short motion has been used. This type of motion can change a one-running-back set to a two-back set or change a two-back set to a three-running-back set. The offensive advantage of short motion is that it changes the flank and could cause an adjustment error by the defense. Both two-step and short motion give an illusion that flow will go in the direction of motion. When the defense adjusts to this motion or concentrates too intently on it, the Wing-T misdirection game can become very effective.

The third type of motion, and the one that has the greatest effect on the defensive team, is extended motion. Like the other motions, it is primarily used by the halfbacks from any of their three basic alignments. The fullback rarely makes use of any type of motion. The main purpose of this motion is to spread the defense by widening the offensive flank on either side. This motion may go through the position of the ball or away from the ball. In either situation, the defense is presented with the problem of an additional wide receiver. (Diagrams 1-6, 1-7)

DIAGRAM 1-6

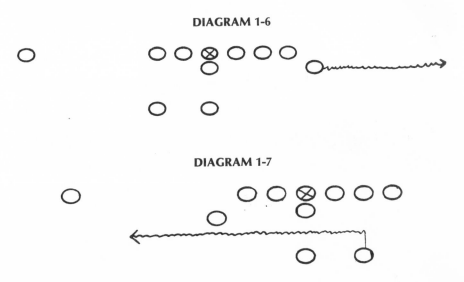

DIAGRAM 1-7

When extended motion is employed by the setback, four quick receivers, on or near the line of scrimmage, are available to the offense. This additional problem must be recognized and handled by the defensive coach. The increased use of extended motion, particularly by the setback, is one reason many defensive coaches feel a four-deep secondary is best versus the Wing-T.

Multiple Threats on All Plays

The backfield action on all Wing-T running plays presents multiple threats to the defense. On every play, the Wing-T attempts, by backfield action, to convince the defense that any one of two or three backs could be carrying the ball. This defensive problem is further complicated because these two or three possible ballcarriers attack different areas along the line of scrimmage. The quarterback presents a constant threat to a flank. He either threatens the playside flank with an Option or Play-Action Pass fake or attacks the offside by faking the Waggle Pass or Run. This excellent use of backfield fakes limits the keying of offensive backs and forces the defensive coach to search for other keys.

An analysis of the Wing-T Sweep clearly reveals its multiple threat approach. (Diagram 1-8) The initial threat is the fullback up the middle on a Dive. The quarterback open pivots to the midline, on his path to mesh with and handoff to the halfback. The fullback passes the quarterback and is responsible for making a good fake. The quarterback makes no fake to the fullback. The nearness of their paths and the fake of the fullback create the illusion of a handoff. The setback receives the ball and attacks the onside flank. The quarterback attacks the offside flank with the threat of a Waggle Pass or Run. Three areas along the line of scrimmage are threatened on one play.

DIAGRAM 1-8

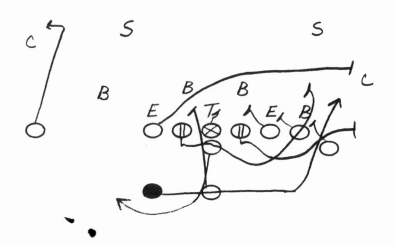

Series Offense

Like most successful offensive schemes, the Wing-T employs a series offense. It uses several different series, each having a base play accompanied by companion plays. The companion plays are designed to take advantage of a defender who, while reacting to stop one play, puts himself in a vulnerable position for another play. The idea is to take advantage of any defensive adjustment used to stop one play. The following analysis of several plays in the Sweep Series illustrates the value of these companion plays.

As explained earlier, the Sweep is designed to attack the playside flank while threatening two other areas. Suppose the onside defensive end, versus the Sweep, does not step down with the inside move of the offensive tackle. Instead, he goes upfield on the snap of the ball. He eludes the attempted inside block by the tight end and avoids the onside guard. He fires directly into the backfield and tackles the halfback for a significant loss. Two companion plays of the Sweep take advantage of the overly aggressive defensive end. (Diagram 1-9)

Giving the ball to the fullback and employing a gut blocking scheme is one alternative. The defensive end sees the same inside move by the offensive tackle, the same pull by the onside guard, and the same backfield action.

DIAGRAM 1-9

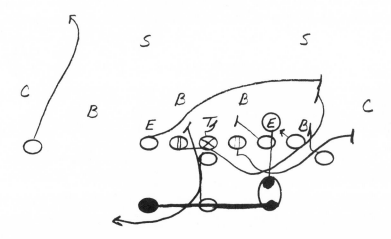

However, the ball is given to the fullback and faked to the halfback. The defensive end takes himself out of the play, and there is no need to even block him. In addition, the influence pull by the onside guard should encourage the onside linebacker to step slightly outside and give the offside guard an excellent blocking angle. (Diagram 1-10)

DIAGRAM 1-10

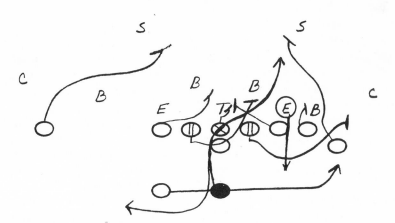

The second alternative is to give the ball to the fullback and use a trap blocking scheme. The defensive end sees the same inside move by the offensive tackle and the same backfield action. Since he does not see the onside guard pull, he slows his charge enough to set himself up for the trap block of the offside guard. The onside linebacker should step up on the down block of the onside guard. This gives the tackle a fine blocking angle on him. Again, the ball is given to the fullback and faked to the halfback. The down block of the onside guard should encourage the onside linebacker to step up and be blocked by the offensive tackle. (Diagram 1-11)

DIAGRAM 1-11

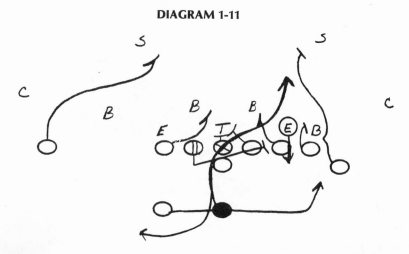

Misdirection Game

The misdirection game is a vital part of the Wing-T series offense and it presents the defense with another dilemma. The ever-present possibility of the counter play may hold defenders longer than necessary and reduce pursuit on flow plays. On the other hand, misdirection plays take advantage of those defenders who become vulnerable by overreacting to flow. Linebackers, at times, pursue too quickly and disregard the possibility of a misdirection play. Defensive linemen may overpenetrate and pursue on the wrong angle and become susceptible to the counterattack. Both overpursuit and overpenetration are exploited by the HB Counter.

The HB Counter is part of the Belly Series and, unlike the companion plays previously described (Fullback Gut and Fullback Trap), the ball is run opposite the backfield flow. Short motion by the wing is often used to initiate the idea of flow and create the possibility of an Option or Play-Action Pass in the direction of the motion. On the snap of the ball, backfield flow goes in the same direction as the motion. The quarterback reverse pivots toward the fullback as he dives to the offside guard-tackle gap. This appears to the defense to be the Belly play. Even the setback "rocks" in the direction of flow before running his inside counter action. After the handoff, the quarterback continues to the side of backfield flow and fakes a Play-Action Pass.

The blocking scheme takes advantage of the overreacting defenders. The onside tackle steps inside and blocks the onside linebacker who erroneously moved too quickly with backfield flow. The overpenetrated defensive end is either trapped by the offside tackle or, if too far upfield, disregarded, and the tackle turns up in the hole as a lead blocker. (Diagram 1-12)

DIAGRAM 1-12

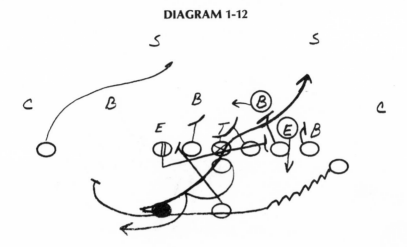

Run-Oriented Passing Game

Like the misdirection game, the run-oriented passing game is another facet of the series approach to offense. The Play-Action Pass takes advantage of those linebackers and defensive backs who overreact to the running game. Like the misdirection game, the run-oriented passing game causes another dilemma. The possibility of a Play-Action Pass may cause the secondary and linebackers to react too slowly to run. However, when the secondary and linebackers react too quickly to run, they become vulnerable to the Play-Action Pass. The Waggle is a companion play to the Sweep and is the cornerstone of the Wing-T Play-Action Passing Game.

The Waggle is part of the Sweep Series and the backfield action is the same as the Sweep and the Fullback Dive. The quarterback keeps the ball after faking to the halfback, while the guards pull opposite the backfield flow to provide protection for the quarterback. Like most Wing-T Play-Action Passes, the quarterback has the option of running or passing as he attacks the onside flank. There are five potential receivers, four of whom employ essential run fakes prior to running their pass patterns.

The tight end and wing step inside to simulate Sweep and then release on their pass routes. The wing occupies the deep outside area, opposite the direction of the quarterback. He is open when the secondary defender, who is responsible for that area, reacts up to the Sweep fake. The tight end drags across the middle and reads the reaction of the secondary defender responsible for that area. When the defender reacts up to the run fake, the tight end breaks behind him and is open for a deep reception. When the deep defender does not react up, the tight end could be open in the linebacker area if they overreact to the Dive or Sweep fake.

The fullback fakes Dive and, if there is no defender in the onside guard-center gap, runs his pattern in the flat. When the defender responsible for that area reacts up to stop the quarterback, the fullback is open.

The halfback fakes Sweep and blocks to the offside. When there is no defender to block, he continues into the offside flat and occupies that area as a potential receiver. Normally, the halfback finds someone to block and does not become a possible pass receiver.

The split end runs the same route that he uses when the Sweep is run. The deep outside defender normally stays in his area of responsibility and covers the split end.

The quarterback executes the Waggle and his decision to run or pass is determined by the way the flank is defended. When he decides to pass, he scans the field, from the onside to the offside, looking for the vulnerable pass defender and the open receiver. (Diagram 1-13)

DIAGRAM 1-13

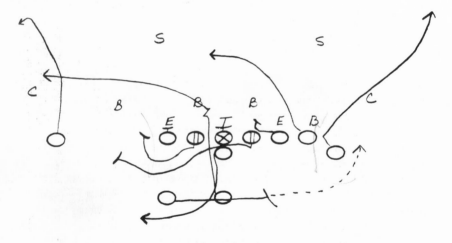

WEAKNESSES

Strong Formation Tendencies

The Wing-T Offense uses many pre-snap alignments and numerous shifts and motions, but at the time the ball is snapped, only one of six basic formations is normally employed. From each of these six formations, only certain plays can be executed. Each Wing-T opponent may use several formation variations and attempt a few different plays, but the plays from the six basic formations make up the bulk of the offense. A thorough understanding of which plays can be run from each basic formation is extremely important. The basic formation-play tendencies are a definite weakness and the basis upon which the defensive coach may begin a successful game plan.

The two most basic formations are the Wing and Slot sets. All other basic Wing-T formations begin with one of these two sets or, prior to the snap of the ball, end up in one of them.

A study of each of the six basic formations and the plays run from each gives an excellent understanding of this formation-play relationship. (Diagrams 1-14, 1-15)

Exceptional Athletic Ability and Versatility at Certain Positions

All offensive schemes need good athletes to be successful. The Wing-T is certainly no exception to this rule. However, the Wing-T not only requires good athletes but also, at certain positions, it must have athletes who are extremely versatile. This is particularly true of the guards and halfbacks.

The guards are expected to master numerous skills. They must possess the size and strength to be effective pass protectors and drive blockers. They must also have the quickness and agility to properly execute the various pulling techniques.

A look at the jobs of guards in other offensive systems gives insight into the degree of athletic ability and versatility required of the Wing-T guards. Even though the Wishbone guards may occasionally have to pull or pass protect, their main job is to be very good drive blockers. The Pro Offense requires guards who are excellent pass protectors, who pull and drive block on occasion. The skills of the Wing-T guards would allow them to perform well in any offensive system. Guards from other offenses could have a very difficult time attempting to master the skills required of the Wing-T guards.

The halfbacks, as discussed earlier in this chapter, must be equally adept at blocking, receiving, and running. Unlike other offenses, where the halfbacks are primarily runners who occasionally block or catch, the Wing-T halfbacks perform all three tasks equally.

The ideal Wing-T Offense has both guards and halfbacks who can perform all their jobs with equal proficiency. However, this is a rare situation. One may be much better than any other at a particular skill or, even worse, only one may adequately perform the necessary task. This may force the offensive team to use that player whenever the particular task is required.

Suppose one guard executes the short trap pull much better than any other guard. If the offensive coach flip-flops this guard to perform the task or traps to only one side, it is an excellent key for the defensive coach.

When one of the halfbacks averages many more carries per game than any other halfback, it is a sure bet he is the best rusher. The defensive coach can take this into consideration when developing the defensive game plan.

Formation tendencies, along with the various employments of particular players, provide excellent information upon which the defensive coach can begin his plan to stop the Wing-T.

DIAGRAM 1-14
SLOT FORMATION PLAYS

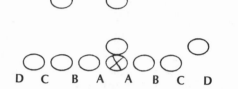

D C B A A B C D

TIGHT-END SIDE PLAYS

B-C: No-Motion Belly
C : Counter Criss-Cross
C-D: Sprint Option
D : Waggle Pass/Run
Sprint-Out Pass

SPLIT-END SIDE PLAYS

A-B: FB Trap
C-D: Sprint Option
C-D: Trap Option
D : Buck Sweep
Sweep Pass
Trap Option Pass
Sprint-Out Pass

SLOT SHORT-MOTION PLAYS

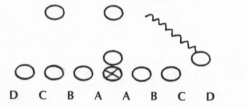

D C B A A B C D

TIGHT-END SIDE PLAYS

A-B: FB Trap
A-B: Slot Counter
B-C: Belly
C-D: Belly Option
D : Slot Sweep
Belly Pass
HB Counter Pass

SPLIT-END SIDE PLAYS

A-B: HB Counter
D : Waggle Pass/Run
Slot Counter-Bootleg Pass

SLOT SETBACK-MOTION PLAYS

D C B A A B C D

TIGHT-END SIDE PLAYS

A : Slot Trap

SPLIT-END SIDE PLAYS

C : Belly
C-D: Belly Option
Belly Pass

DIAGRAM 1-15
WING FORMATION PLAYS

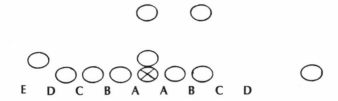

E   D   C   B   A   A   B   C   D

TIGHT-END SIDE PLAYS

A-B: FB Trap
C : Off-Tackle
C : Power
D : Buck Sweep
D : Lead Sweep
Sweep Pass
Sprint-Out Pass

SPLIT-END SIDE PLAYS

B-C: No-Motion Belly
C : Counter Criss-Cross
C-D: Sprint Option
D : Waggle Pass/Run
Sprint-Out Pass

WING SHORT-MOTION PLAYS

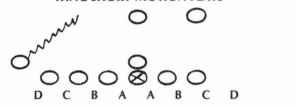

D   C   B   A   A   B   C   D

TIGHT-END SIDE PLAYS

A-B: HB Counter
D : Waggle Pass/Run
Wing Counter-Bootleg Pass

SPLIT-END SIDE PLAYS

A-B: FB Trap
A-B: Wing Counter
B-C: Belly
C-D: Belly Option
D : Wing Sweep
Belly Pass
HB Counter Pass

WING SETBACK-MOTION PLAYS

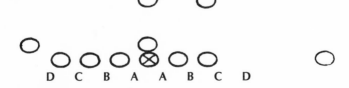

D   C   B   A   A   B   C   D

TIGHT-END SIDE PLAYS

C : Belly Down
C-D: Belly Option
Belly Pass

SPLIT-END SIDE PLAYS

A : Wing Trap

Summary of Key Points

1. The placement of the halfback in a Wing or Slot position creates additional problems for the defense.

2. The offense employs a three-running-back attack with one, two, or three backs in the backfield with equal frequency.

3. The use of pre-snap shifts and motions allows the offense a multiplicity of formations.

4. Backfield actions on all running plays present multiple threats to the defense.

5. The series approach to offense employs companion plays, misdirection plays, and Play-Action Passes to take advantage of those defenders who overreact to various facets of the running game.

6. Strong formation-play tendencies are a definite weakness of the offense and a key for defenders.

7. The need for extremely versatile athletes at certain positions may cause the placement of one athlete in various positions and create a noticeable offensive tendency.

Chapter 2

Installing the
3-4 Slant

Our 3-4 defensive package, like all well-constructed defensive systems, is designed to be effective against all possible offensive schemes. Unlike many defensive systems, our 3-4 is uncomplicated to teach and learn. However, it presents many unique problems for our opponents to solve.

The 3-4 Slant is only one facet of our 3-4 package. It was developed primarily to defend against the Wing-T but is applicable against any offense. This is particularly true when the defensive team has acquired strong formation tendencies on the opponent.

BASIC DEFENSIVE CONCEPTS

Reasons for the 3-4 Front

For the defensive team, the most reliable Wing-T key is the offensive line and particularly the guards. To take advantage of this key, the inside linebackers must be placed in a position where they have an unobstructed view of the guards. The 3-4 puts them in this position.

Stopping the FB Trap and the HB Counter is an extremely important element in defending against the Wing-T running attack. The use of a nose tackle nearly guarantees a down block by the onside guard on both plays. This provides an excellent key for the onside linebacker.

The use of a nose tackle also forces the center into many one-on-one blocks. Blocking a down lineman on his nose is a much more difficult task than blocking a linebacker over him in an even front.

When the FB Dive is run with a gut blocking scheme, the center is forced to one-on-one block the nose tackle. The false pull by the onside guard, coupled with the Sweep backfield action, influences the onside linebacker to step outside. The odd front forces the center to single block the nose tackle until the onside tackle can get down to help. The pull of the offside guard gives the offside linebacker a very good key and takes him to the point of attack. Without a quality one-on-one block by the center, the chance for a successful play is very doubtful. (Diagram 2-1)

DIAGRAM 2-1

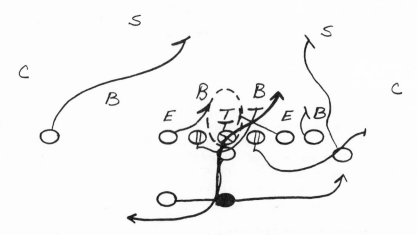

Reasons for Four-Deep Secondary

Flexibility is the most important reason for the employment of a four-deep secondary. The use of four athletes who are capable of defending against the pass, as well as being effective run-support personnel, provides defensive versatility. The defense has the ability to employ numerous zone, man-to-man, and combination coverages. The four-deep creates the ever-present possibility of a secondary blitz. This is an important weapon for the defense and an additional problem for the offense.

The ever-increasing use of the passing game and the deployment of two, three, and four receivers, on or near the line of scrimmage, forces defensive adjustments. The use of four defensive backs facilitates these adjustments and allows athletes of similar speed and ability to cover these receivers and defend against the passing game.

Versus the run, the four-deep secondary provides an extra defender to the side of the run while still protecting the three deep zones for any Play-Action Passes. The three defensive backs in the deep areas are also in an excellent position to pursue the play and protect against cutbacks. (Diagram 2-2)

DIAGRAM 2-2

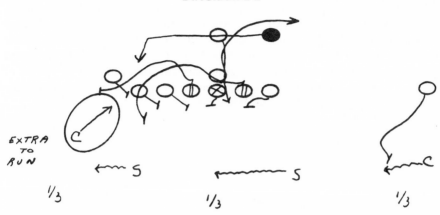

Unlike a three-deep secondary, the four-deep makes use of two safeties. Both safeties are in a good position to attack a running play from the inside-out. Versus a run, one may become the extra run defender while the other protects the deep middle zone for any Play-Action Pass before getting into the correct angle of pursuit. (Diagram 2-3)

DIAGRAM 2-3

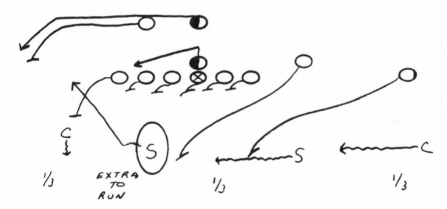

Reasons for No Personnel "Flip-Flopping"

The Wing-T Offense employs pre-snap shifts to take advantage of defensive teams who use weakside and strongside personnel. The change of strength forces this defense to either shift personnel with the change or play defenders out of position.

The way to eliminate this defensive dilemma is to teach all defenders to play against the weakside and strongside of an offense. For example, when coaching the safeties, there is no need to differentiate between a strong and a free safety. All safeties are taught the techniques required to play both positions. Therefore, when offensive strength changes, there is no need to flip-flop the safeties, and neither one is playing out of position.

Normally, when the offensive coach sees there is no advantage to be gained by pre-snap shifts, they are no longer used.

SLANT FRONT CALLS

The term "Slant" is called in the defensive huddle. The direction of the slant is not determined until the offensive team aligns over the ball. The direction is based on the play tendencies of the particular offensive formation employed. Unless the Wing-T opponent has developed formation-play tendencies contrary to those in Diagrams 1-14 and 1-15, we use the following basic direction calls:

1. Versus a wing - Slant to the wing.

2. Versus a slot - Slant to the slot.

3. Versus motion - Slant in the direction the motion is going.

The defensive front must listen for directional change calls. When the offensive team shifts or employs motion, the original call may no longer be applicable and a second, or even a third, call may be required. Every day, the week prior to playing a Wing-T opponent, it is vital for the defensive front to practice these change-of-direction calls.

An inside linebacker makes the directional call. His first call is "Wing Right or Left" or "Slot Right or Left." Once a shift occurs, he may change the directional call. When motion is used, he calls "Motion Right or Left" and the front reacts accordingly. The only significant call is the last call.

ALIGNMENT AND PLAY
OF THE DEFENSIVE FRONT

Tackle and Ends

The basic alignment of the nose tackle is head-on the center, while the end aligns head-on the offensive tackle. The end may vary his alignment slightly in an attempt to disguise his intention to slant. However, he must not vary his alignment to a point where he cannot effectively slant to his target point. He aligns as deep as necessary to prevent the offensive player, on whom he is aligned, from cutting him off when he executes the slant.

The slant is executed toward a target point. The target point is the nose of the offensive player to the immediate right (Slant Right) or left (Slant Left) of the offensive player on whom the defender is aligned. When slanting to an area where there is no offensive player, the defender slants to an imaginary target point on an imaginary player. This occurs when the end slants to an offensive end or slot who is split more than two yards from the offensive tackle. The end slants to a place where a normal tight end would align. (Diagram 2-4)

DIAGRAM 2-4

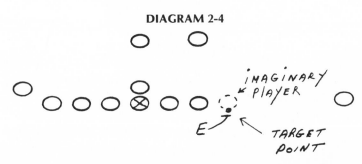

The defenders attempt to get a piece of the offensive players to whom they are slanting. They read their movements and react to them. They are very conscious of not penetrating too deeply into the backfield and becoming susceptible to a trap or kick-out block.

The reads and reactions of the three defensive linemen are very similar and simple, allowing the defensive coach the flexibility of interchanging the personnel playing these three positions.

The defenders' keys are the offensive players to whom they are slanting. The nose tackle and offside end (end away from the call) read the guard to whom they are slanting. The onside end (end to the side of the call) reads the tight end or slot. The reads are as follows:

1. The key blocks the slanting defender. The defender goes across the face of the blocker and fights through the block. (Diagram 2-5)

2. The key blocks straight ahead, attempting to block the inside linebacker. The onside end does not get involved with this block. The defender jams the guard, not allowing him to get to the linebacker. He gets his head to the side of the ball. (Diagram 2-6)

DIAGRAM 2-5   **DIAGRAM 2-6**

Slant left for all Diagrams 2-5 to 2-13.

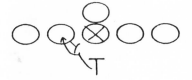

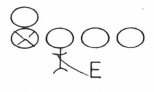

3. The key blocks opposite the slanting defender. The defender keeps his offside arm out, feeling for a block by the offensive player on whom he was originally aligned. When no block comes from that player, he looks for a fold block (Diagram 2-7), a lead block (Diagram 2-8), or a trap block (Diagram 2-9).

DIAGRAM 2-7   **DIAGRAM 2-8**

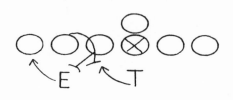

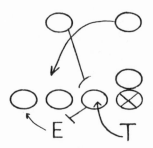

DIAGRAM 2-9

4. The key pulls. This only affects the onside end when the tight end or slot pulls inside. The defender gets in the "hip pocket" of the pulling player and runs with him, parallel to the line of scrimmage. (Diagram 2-10)

5. The key sets up to pass block. The defender executes the slant and rushes the passer. (Diagram 2-11)

DIAGRAM 2-10   **DIAGRAM 2-11**

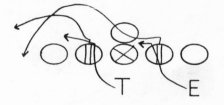

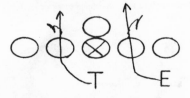

Unlike the nose tackle and the offside end, the onside end has a few additional reads particular to his position. These are as follows:

1. The tight end or slot releases for a pass. The onside end attempts to jam him but does not go wider than the original target point. (Diagram 2-12)

2. The onside end slants to an end or slot split over two yards. He slants to an imaginary player and looks to the near back. He squeezes any block, by the back, and keeps outside leverage on the ball. (Diagram 2-13)

DIAGRAM 2-12

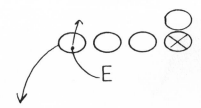

DIAGRAM 2-13

Inside Linebackers

The inside linebacker aligns with his nose on the outside ear of the offensive guard. His depth is determined by the down and distance. He may align as shallow as two yards off the ball or as deep as five.

The reads and reactions, used by the inside linebacker when Slant is employed, are the same as those used with our 3-4 package. Very little additional teaching or learning is required. The primary key is the offensive guard on whom the linebacker is aligned. Initially, he reads the movements of the guard and reacts to them. After the primary read, the second key is the near offensive back. The use of a second key helps eliminate the potential problems caused by an influence pull by the guard.

The primary reads are as follows:

1. The key blocks down. The linebacker steps up and slightly outside. He steps outside to prevent a down block by the offensive tackle

when a trapping scheme is used. (Diagram 2-14) He also looks for a lead block. (Diagram 2-15) He maintains outside leverage on the ball.

DIAGRAM 2-14

DIAGRAM 2-15

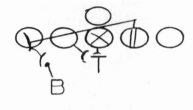

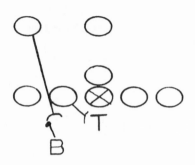

2. The key blocks straight ahead. The linebacker steps up and attacks the blocker with his inside arm, keeping outside leverage. (Diagram 2-16)

3. The key attempts to cut the linebacker off. He goes across the face of the guard and fights through the block. (Diagram 2-17)

DIAGRAM 2-16

DIAGRAM 2-17

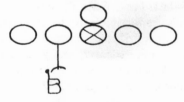

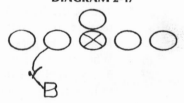

4. The key blocks outside. The linebacker steps up to meet a fold block (Diagram 2-18) or a lead block. (Diagram 2-19)

DIAGRAM 2-18

DIAGRAM 2-19

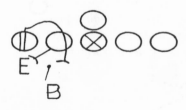

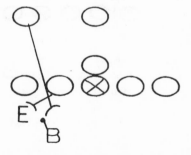

5. The key pulls. The linebacker steps parallel to the line of scrimmage with the key. He takes only one step before reading his backfield key. This prevents being taken out of position by an influence pull. (Diagram 2-20)

6. The key sets up to pass block. The linebacker reads the quarterback and gets into his proper zone. (Diagram 2-21)

DIAGRAM 2-20   **DIAGRAM 2-21**

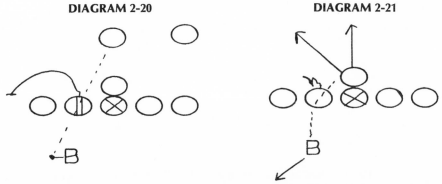

The zone pass coverage responsibilities of the inside linebacker are the same for Slant as our basic 3-4 Package. Once the offense aligns over the ball, the linebacker analyzes the formation to determine the possible receivers who could threaten his zone coverage areas. Once pass is recognized, from either the guard or backfield key, he goes to his zone. His reactions and responsibilities are as follows:

1. The quarterback executes a Drop-Back Pass. When there is a wide receiver to his side, the linebacker's responsibility is the curl area. However, he goes through the hook area first, then proceeds to curl. When there is a receiver in the hook area, he covers that zone until it is vacated and then goes to curl. When there is no wide receiver to his side, his responsibility is the hook zone. (Diagram 2-22)

DIAGRAM 2-22

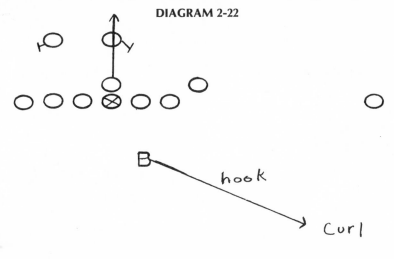

2.   The quarterback's passing action takes him wider than the offensive guard to the linebacker's side. This is the same as Drop-Back for the linebacker.

3.   The quarterback's passing action takes him wider than the offensive guard to the side opposite the linebacker. The linebacker covers the middle hook area, looking for crossing receivers. We refer to this as covering the "hole." (Diagram 2-23)

DIAGRAM 2-23

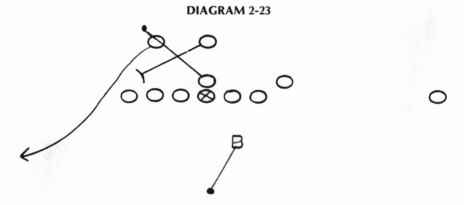

Outside Linebackers

The outside linebacker, to the side of a tight end or tight slot, aligns with his nose on the outside ear of the offensive player. When onside (outside linebacker to the side of the Slant call), he aligns as deep as necessary to prevent the offensive player, on whom he is aligned, from cutting him off when he executes his slant. When offside (outside linebacker away from the Slant call), he aligns as tight to the line of scrimmage as possible.

Versus an end or slot, split over two yards from the offensive tackle, an offside linebacker aligns on an imaginary tight end. An onside linebacker stays in his normal alignment, including depth, until the end or slot splits wider than five yards. He then moves to a walkaway alignment or aligns on an imaginary tight end. In a walkaway, he aligns midway between the offensive tackle and the end or slot at an approximate depth of five yards. (Diagram 2-24)

DIAGRAM 2-24

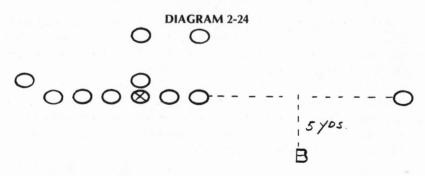

Only the onside linebacker employs a slant technique and only when aligned on a real or imaginary tight end or tight slot. He slants to the next real or imaginary offensive player. When the next real offensive player is split over two yards, the linebacker slants to an imaginary player. (Diagrams 2-25, 2-26)

DIAGRAM 2-25

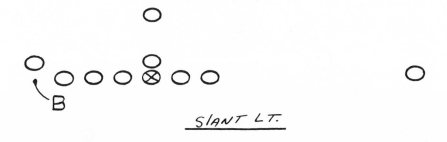

DIAGRAM 2-26

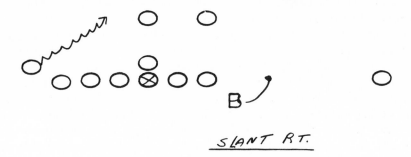

The onside linebacker's main goal, versus the run, is to keep outside leverage on the ball. He fights through the head of any blocker attempting to pin him inside. When aligned in a walkaway, he is particularly aware of a crackback block by a wide receiver to his side.

Versus a pass, he becomes a safety and his responsibility is to cover the curl area, when there is a wide receiver to his side, and then to cover the flat zone. This responsibility is in effect when the quarterback executes a Drop-Back Pass or employs a passing action beyond the offensive guard to the side of the linebacker. (Diagram 2-27)

DIAGRAM 2-27

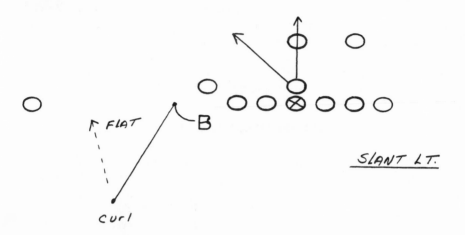

When the quarterback uses a passing action to the opposite side, the onside linebacker employs a "comeback" technique. As he drops into the curl area, he eyeballs the wide receiver to his side. When the receiver runs an inside pattern under fifteen yards, he picks him up man-to-man. When there is no inside pattern, he checks for a back coming out of the backfield to his side. When one comes out, he takes him man-to-man. Where there is no back, he sprints to the deep middle to help out. (Diagram 2-28)

DIAGRAM 2-28

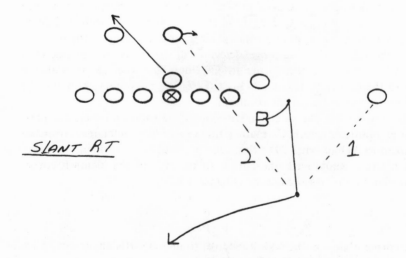

The offside outside linebacker, versus run and pass, executes a blitz. He uses a point one yard in front of the fullback as his target. When aligned on a tight end or tight slot, he goes through the outside shoulder of the offensive player in an attempt to disrupt a pass pattern or an inside block. He executes this blitz with reckless abandon and a great desire to get into the backfield and make a Big Play. This blitz can disrupt many Wing-T plays but has been most effective versus the Sweep, Options and Waggle to the side of the offside linebacker.

ZONE SECONDARY CALLS

"Roll" zone coverage is primarily used in conjunction with a Slant call. It is a rotating three-deep zone with a safety or corner covering the flat zone to the side of the rotation call. The rotation is normally called opposite the direction of the Slant. Therefore, only "Roll" is called in the defensive huddle, and the direction is called when the offensive team aligns over the ball. Like Slant, the direction of the Roll can change when the offensive team uses motions and pre-snap shifts. A safety makes the initial call and any necessary directional change calls.

The Roll, called opposite the Slant, provides perimeter pass coverage in five areas or zones. The three deep zones are protected, while both curl-to-flat zones are covered. To the side of the Slant call, the onside linebacker covers curl-to-flat and the rotating corner or safety covers it to the opposite side. This coverage provides excellent protection against Waggle and is thoroughly discussed, with variations, in Chapter 7.

All four secondary defenders align at a depth of seven yards. We refer to this as a "four-across-the-board" alignment. Since we can execute most of our 3-4 package secondary coverages from this alignment, it is impossible for a quarterback to get a successful pre-snap read. We also hide Roll coverage by aligning in one of our other basic alignments and jumping to the four-across-the-board, or a pre-rotated zone, prior to or at the snap of the ball.

Once the side of the rotation is determined, the safety to that side calls either "Ivy" or "Cup" to the corner to his side. The other safety makes a false call to the corner to his side. This negates the possibility of giving the offense a key as to the side of the rotation.

When Ivy is used, the safety to the side of the rotation covers the curl-to-flat on any passing action. The other three secondary defenders cover the three deep zones. (Diagram 2-29)

When Cup is employed, the corner to the side of the rotation covers the curl-to-flat on any passing action. (Diagram 2-30)

Corners

The corner aligns on the widest receiver to his side. His alignment varies with the split of the receiver. His alignment rules are as follows:

DIAGRAM 2-29

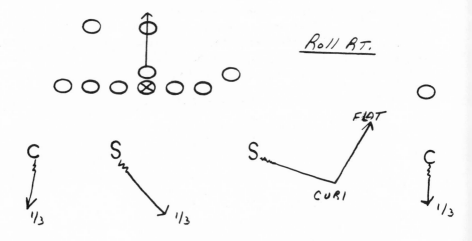

DIAGRAM 2-30

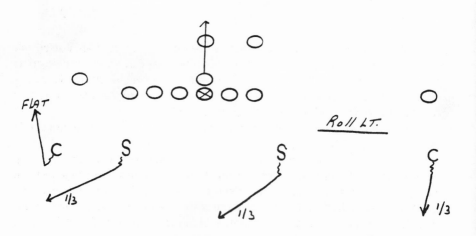

1. Versus a receiver split up to ten yards, the corner aligns one yard outside the receiver.

2. Versus a receiver split over ten yards, the corner aligns with his nose on the outside shoulder of the receiver.

3. When the receiver aligns closer than seven yards to the sideline, the corner aligns seven yards from the sideline.

The corner keys through the widest receiver to the backfield action. As a second key, when his alignment allows, he keys through an uncovered offensive lineman to help determine run or pass.

When Cup is called and it is a pass, the onside corner makes contact with the widest receiver. He attempts to force the receiver inside while looking for a second receiver releasing into the flat area. The offside corner covers the deep outside one-third zone. (Diagram 2-31)

DIAGRAM 2-31

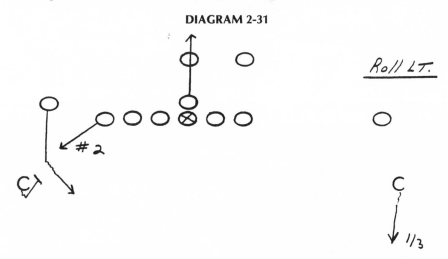

When Cup is called and it is a run, the onside corner does not permit a wide receiver to block him. He attacks the play outside-in and restricts the running lane. He looks for plays to bounce outside. The offside corner checks for Waggle, HB Counter, Reverse, or a Throwback Pass before getting into the proper angle of pursuit. (Diagram 2-32)

When Ivy is called and it is a pass, both corners cover the deep outside one-third zones. (Diagram 2-33)

When Ivy is called and it is a run, the onside corner checks the deep outside one-third zone for a Play-Action Pass. He comes late to support all running plays from the outside-in. When the wide receiver attempts a crack-back block, he yells "Crack" to alert the inside defender and supports right away. The offside corner uses the same technique he used with the Cup call. (Diagram 2-34)

Safeties

The basic alignment of the safety is head-on the tight end or tight slot. When there is no tight end or tight slot, he aligns on an imaginary tight end. However, certain circumstances cause the alignment to vary. The variations in alignment are as follows:

1. Versus a formation with only a tight end to one side and, at least, one wide receiver to the other, the safeties change their alignments.

DIAGRAM 2-32

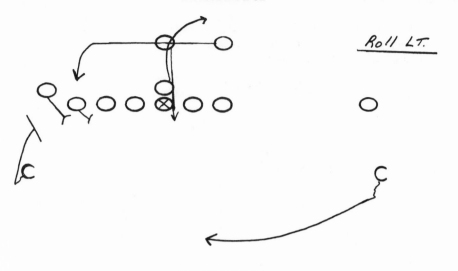

Roll LT.

DIAGRAM 2-33

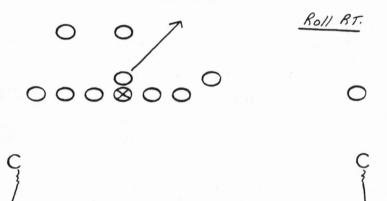

Roll RT.

DIAGRAM 2-34

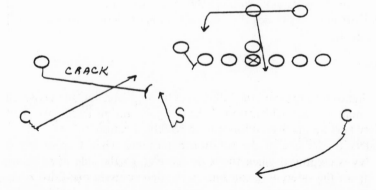

Roll LT.

The safety to the tight-end side aligns head-on the offensive guard to his side. The other safety aligns three yards outside the tight-end position. (Diagram 2-35)

DIAGRAM 2-35

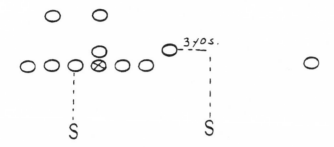

2. When the ball is on the hash mark and strength, with a wide receiver to the field, adjustments are made. The safety to the short side moves head-on the guard to that side. The other safety aligns three yards outside the tight-end position. (Diagram 2-36)

DIAGRAM 2-36

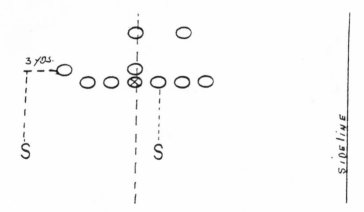

When aligned on a receiver, the safety keys through him and an uncovered offensive lineman to backfield action. When aligned on an imaginary tight end, the safety keys an uncovered lineman to backfield action.

The safety to the side of the rotation determines when Cup or Ivy is to be used. Ivy is employed when the wide receiver, to the side of rotation, is split too far for the safety to cover him in the deep outside one-third zone.

The distance varies with the speed and ability of the safety. When the safety feels he can cover the receiver in the deep zone, he employs Cup.

When Cup is called and it is a pass, the onside safety covers the deep outside one-third zone. The offside safety covers the deep middle one-third zone. (Diagram 2-37)

DIAGRAM 2-37

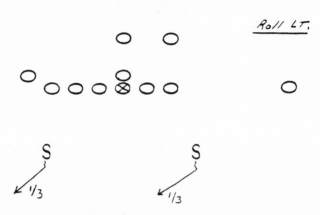

When Cup is called and it is a run, the onside safety checks the deep outside one-third zone for a Play-Action Pass. He comes late to support all running plays from the outside-in. The offside safety mirrors the quarterback, checking the onside wide receiver for a Play-Action Pass before filling. (Diagram 2-38)

DIAGRAM 2-38

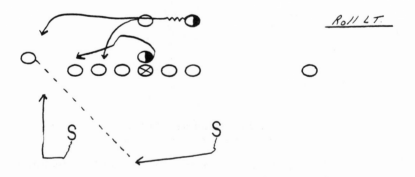

When Ivy is called and it is a pass, the onside safety covers curl-to-flat. The offside safety uses the same technique he used with a Cup call. (Diagram 2-39)

DIAGRAM 2-39

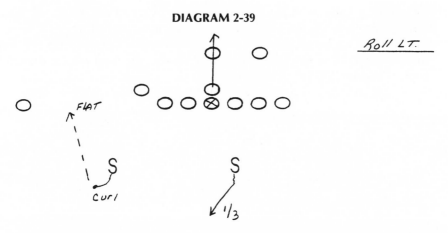

When Ivy is called and it is a run, the onside safety attacks the play from the inside-out. Again, the offside safety uses the same technique he used with a Cup call. (Diagram 2-40)

DIAGRAM 2-40

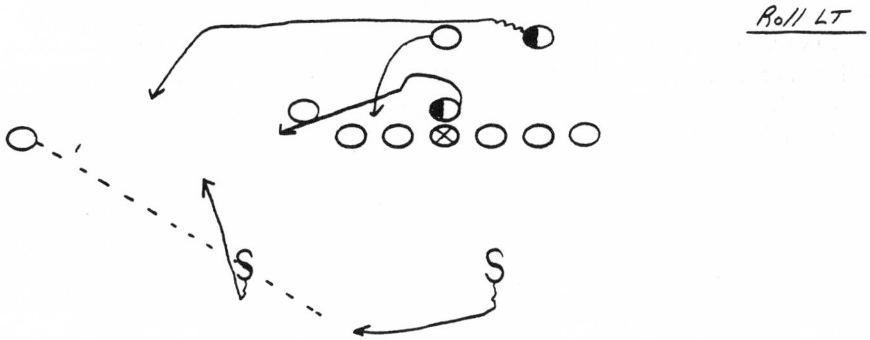

Summary of Key Points

1. The 3-4 Front provides the inside linebackers with an unobstructed view of the best Wing-T keys, the offensive guards.

2. The Four-Deep Secondary allows defensive flexibility while always providing an extra defender to the side of the run.

3. Teaching defensive personnel to play to the weakside and to the strongside eliminates the offensive advantages of pre-snap shifting.

4. The direction of the 3-4 Slant is called when the offensive team aligns over the ball and is determined by the play tendencies of each formation.

5. The nose tackle and ends listen for the last directional change call and slant accordingly.

6. The inside linebackers read and react to the movements of the offensive guards.

7. The onside outside linebacker executes a slant while the offside linebacker employs a blitz.

8. The secondary uses a rotating three-deep zone coverage with either a safety or corner covering the curl-to-flat area to the side of rotation.

9. The side to which the secondary rotates is normally opposite the direction of the Šlant.

10. The safety to the side of rotation ·determines when Cup or Ivy is to be used.

Chapter 3

Installing the 3-4 Read Blitz

The 3-4 Read Blitz is another segment of our 3-4 defense. The Read Blitz was initially developed as a means of attacking a drop-back passer. However, after some experimentation and minor modifications, the Read Blitz became an excellent weapon versus the Wing-T Offense. Unlike the Slant, it is not based on offensive tendencies. Also, pre-snap motions and shifts have little effect on it.

READ BLITZ FRONT CALL

The term "Read Blitz" or "Fake Read Blitz" is called in the defensive huddle. When Fake Read Blitz is called, the inside linebackers align in an Up alignment but move to a normal 3-4 alignment prior to the snap of the ball. The other defenders align in a normal 3-4 alignment.

Since offensive pre-snap motions and shifts have little effect on the defensive front, there is little need for the inside linebackers to call out the position of the wing or slot. However, the linebackers make offensive formation identification calls with all defenses to eliminate the possibility of the offense recognizing when Slant is to be employed.

ALIGNMENT AND PLAY
OF THE DEFENSIVE FRONT

Tackle and Ends

The nose tackle aligns head-on the center, as close to the ball as possible. He aligns close to the ball to keep the center from getting a clean block on either Up inside linebacker. He is responsible for both center-guard gaps. His reads are as follows:

1. The key blocks straight ahead. The nose plays square on the center, not taking a side until he sees the ball or feels the pressure of an inside block (double-team) by either guard. (Diagram 3-1)

2. The key puts his head to either side of the defender. The nose goes across the face of the blocker, fighting through his head. (Diagram 3-2)

DIAGRAM 3-1   **DIAGRAM 3-2**

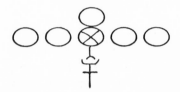   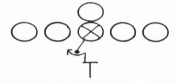

3. The key blocks offside, attempting to block the Up linebacker. The nose jams the center and steps offside with him, keeping him off the Up linebacker. He is careful not to go too far offside, giving the onside guard an easy down block. His onside foot does not go farther offside than the original alignment of his offside foot. (Diagram 3-3)

4. The key sets up to pass block. The nose rushes the passer, staying alert for a Middle Screen or Draw. (Diagram 3-4)

DIAGRAM 3-3   **DIAGRAM 3-4**

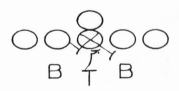   

The end aligns with his nose on the outside ear of the offensive tackle, as close to the line of scrimmage as possible. He aligns close to the line of scrimmage for the same reason as the nose tackle - he wants to prevent a clean inside block by the offensive tackle on the Up inside linebacker. He is responsible for the tackle-end gap. His reads are as follows:

1. The key puts his head to either side of the defender. The end goes across the face of the blocker, fighting through his head. (Diagram 3-5)

DIAGRAM 3-5

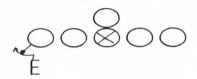

2. The key blocks inside, attempting to block the Up linebacker. The end jams the tackle and squeezes inside, keeping the tackle off the Up linebacker. He is careful not to go too far inside, giving an outside blocker the opportunity to block him inside on a Sweep. His onside foot does not go farther inside than the original alignment of his inside foot. (Diagrams 3-6, 3-7, 3-8) He is constantly aware of a trap block by the offside guard or tackle. He is careful not to overpenetrate and become vulnerable to this block. (Diagram 3-9)

DIAGRAM 3-6

DIAGRAM 3-7

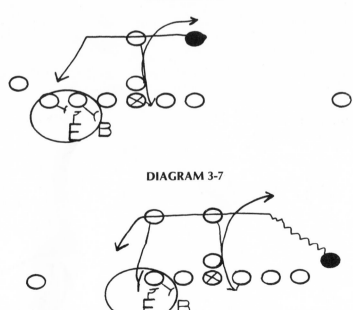

DIAGRAM 3-8

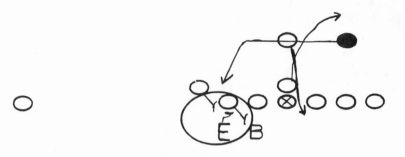

DIAGRAM 3-9

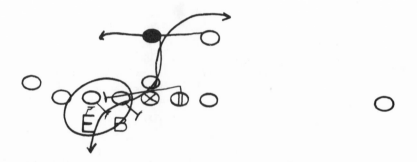

3. The key pulls. The end gets in the "hip pocket" of the tackle and runs with him, parallel to the line of scrimmage. (Diagram 3-10)

4. The key sets up to pass block. The end rushes the passer from the outside-in.

DIAGRAM 3-10

The Inside Linebackers

The inside linebacker aligns with his nose on the outside ear of the offensive guard, as close to the line of scrimmage as possible. He employs his normal two-point stance and the guard remains his initial key. This is called the Up alignment.

In the Up alignment, the linebacker is primarily a run defender and a pass rusher. On the snap of the ball, he steps with his inside foot and attempts to get his hands on the shoulders of the guard. He employs the same reads versus the guard that the end uses against the tackle. However, there are a few significant differences, and these are the basis for the Read Blitz defense. Two of the three major differences are as follows:

1. The key pulls outside. The defender blitzes behind the pull and uses a point one yard in front and two yards to his side of the fullback as his target. (Diagram 3-11)

DIAGRAM 3-11

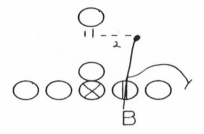

2. The key pulls inside. The defender blitzes behind the pull and uses a point one yard in front of the fullback as his target. (Diagram 3-12)

DIAGRAM 3-12

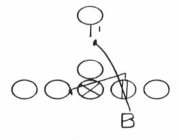

The most significant difference in the way the Up linebacker and end read and react to a key occurs when the key sets up to pass block. Unlike the end, the linebacker may wind up in pass coverage.

Once the linebacker gets his hands on the guard's shoulders and recognizes a pass block, he pushes off and sprints to his zone coverage area. This leaves the guard in an ineffective position, particularly on a Drop-Back Pass. It is too late for him to go outside and pick up the blitzing outside linebacker. His only viable alternative is to help inside, and he may be too far out of position even to help there. The offense is left with two possible alternatives to prevent a quarterback sack. Either a back must be kept in to pick up the blitzing outside linebacker, or the ball must be thrown before the blitzer reaches the quarterback. (Diagram 3-13)

DIAGRAM 3-13

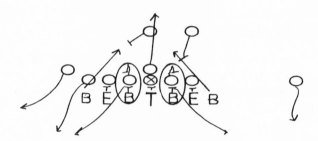

The offensive coach may choose to pull the offensive guard to pick up the blitzing outside linebacker. The offensive dilemma remains the same. Either a back must remain to pick up the inside linebacker, or the quarterback must get rid of the ball very quickly. (Diagram 3-14)

DIAGRAM 3-14

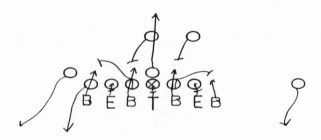

Since we delay the release of all receivers and play a tight man-to-man pass coverage, the only way the offense can hope to prevent a sack is to keep the setbacks in as blockers. This nearly guarantees a three-receiver pass pattern. (Diagram 3-15)

DIAGRAM 3-15

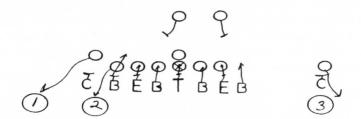

The Outside Linebackers

The outside linebacker executes the same alignment and technique that the offside outside linebacker employs when Slant is used. However, unlike Slant, he is not the defender responsible for outside contain. (Diagram 3-16)

DIAGRAM 3-16

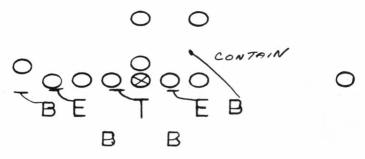

SlANT LEFT

When Read Blitz is employed, it is the responsibility of the end to contain the quarterback. This allows the linebacker to execute his blitz with even more recklessness. (Diagram 3-17)

DIAGRAM 3-17

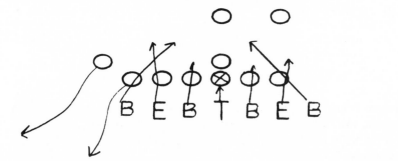

HE-MAN SECONDARY CALL

"He-Man" is a form of man-to-man pass coverage used only with Read Blitz. This coverage has the capability of being pure man-to-man or man-to-man with a free safety. This is determined by the number of receivers involved in the pattern. When three receivers release, which is the normal case when Read Blitz is employed, one of the safeties becomes free. If four receivers release, all four defensive backs play pure man-to-man coverage.

Like our zone coverages, the secondary can use various pre-snap alignments to disguise this coverage.

Corners

Like our zone coverages, the corner aligns on the widest receiver to his side. This receiver is known as number one. He aligns as tight to the receiver as possible when he is not covered by an outside linebacker. This is our lock-on technique.

The corner varies his position on number one according to his split. His alignment rules are as follows:

1. Versus a number one who is covered by an outside linebacker, he aligns with his nose on the outside ear of number one at a depth of four to five yards. (Diagram 3-18)

DIAGRAM 3-18

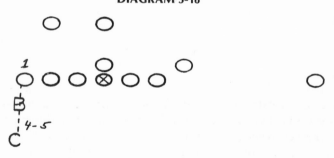

2. Versus a number one split up to five yards, and not covered by an outside linebacker, he aligns with his nose on the outside ear of the receiver. When the receiver releases, he jams him and funnels him inside. (Diagram 3-19)

3. Versus a number one split over five yards, he aligns with his nose on the inside ear of the receiver. When he releases, he jams him and forces him outside. (Diagram 3-20)

4. Versus a number one who employs short or extended motion, he bumps inside to the next receiver. This receiver becomes the widest receiver or number one. (Diagram 3-21)

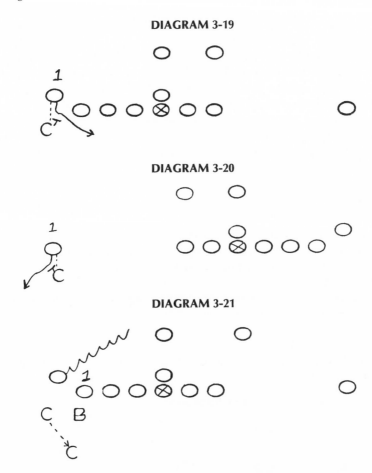

DIAGRAM 3-19

DIAGRAM 3-20

DIAGRAM 3-21

When the key releases, the corner covers him until the ball is thrown or a definite running play is recognized. Once a running play is diagnosed, he does not leave his receiver until the ball crosses the line of scrimmage.

When the key blocks, the corner cannot react up to run too quickly. He checks for a delay route by the receiver. When all threats of a pass are gone, he attacks the running play from the outside-in. When the ball is run away from him, he gets into his proper pursuit angle.

Safeties

Since the corner is responsible for the widest receiver, the safety covers the second receiver from the outside-in. This receiver is known as number two. The alignment of the safety is determined by the position of number two. The various alignments of number two and the safety are as follows:

1. Versus a number two who is covered by an outside linebacker, he

aligns with his nose on the outside ear of number two at a depth of four to five yards. (Diagram 3-22)

DIAGRAM 3-22

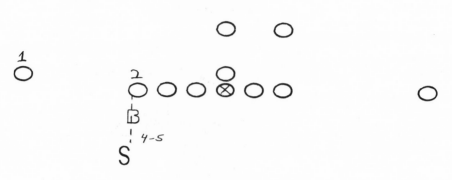

2.   Versus a split number two, who is not covered by an outside linebacker, the safety uses the same alignment rules employed by the corner versus a split number one. (Diagrams 3-23, 3-24)

DIAGRAM 3-23

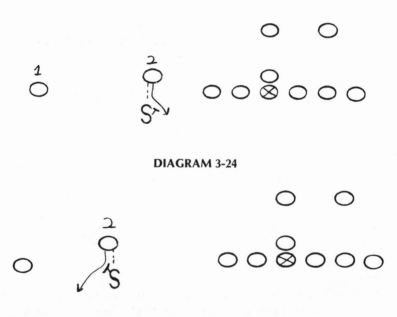

DIAGRAM 3-24

3.   Versus a number two who employs short or extended motion, the safety moves to a position five to six yards over the near offensive tackle. Since he is still responsible for the number two receiver, he looks to the fullback as the possible number two. When the fullback becomes number two, he picks him up man-to-man. (Diagram 3-

25) When there is no number two, the safety becomes free. (Diagram 3-26)

DIAGRAM 3-25

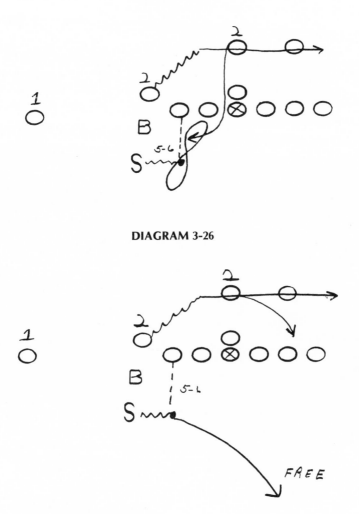

DIAGRAM 3-26

4.   Versus a number two who is aligned as a setback, the safety aligns over the near offensive tackle at a depth of five to six yards. When number two comes out to his side, the safety takes him man-to-man. (Diagram 3-27) When number two goes away, he looks to the fullback. When the fullback becomes number two, he picks him up man-to-man. When there is no number two, the safety becomes free.

DIAGRAM 3-27

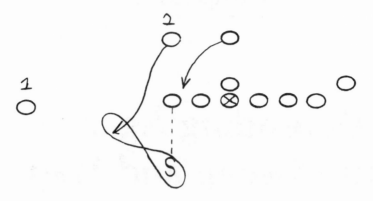

When his receiver (key) releases, the safety plays his man in the same manner as the corner. Unlike the corner, he attacks all running plays from the outside-in.

Summary of Key Points

1. Unlike Slant, the Read Blitz is not based on offensive tendencies.

2. The Read Blitz, which was originally designed to stop the drop-back passer, provides the possibility of a seven-man pass rush.

3. The nose tackle, end, and outside linebacker align in a normal 3-4 alignment.

4. The inside linebacker employs an Up alignment.

5. The Up alignment and actions of the inside linebackers force the offense to keep backs in to protect the passer.

6. Normally, only three receivers can safely release versus the Read Blitz.

7. The He-Man secondary coverage is pure man-to-man versus four receivers and man-to-man with a free safety versus three.

Chapter 4

Defending Against
the Sweep and Trap

In Chapters 4 through 9, the Slant and Read Blitz are described against the basic Wing-T plays. The offensive plays and formations used in these chapters are based on Diagrams 1-14 and 1-15. These plays, and others, may be executed from different formations. However, these chapters deal with the basic Wing-T plays from the basic Wing-T formations. Chapter 10 deals with current play and formation variations.

THE SWEEP FROM VARIOUS FORMATIONS

Along with various Options and the Waggle, the Buck Sweep is a prime method of attacking the flank. As described in Chapter 1, the Sweep makes use of the multiple threat approach to offense. Both flanks and the middle are threatened by one play. The onside flank is threatened by the halfback, while the fullback threatens the middle. The offside flank is attacked by the quarterback.

There are two formation requirements for running the Sweep. The play is executed to a flank with a setback, slot, or wing to that side. This eliminates the possibility of running the play to a flank where the halfback employed motion toward the opposite flank. Second, a halfback must be in a position, either by motion or set, to receive the handoff.

Using the Slant

Both inside linebackers step in the direction of the pulling guards and then look into the backfield for a flow key. The crossing action of the fullback

47

and offside halfback momentarily delays the offside linebacker. He checks for Fullback Dive with either a trap blocking or influence-pull scheme. When he is sure the fullback does not have the ball, he pursues the play.

The onside linebacker flows with the guard pull and the action of the ballcarrier. He fires through the first opening where he feels he can make the tackle.

The nose tackle slants into the area vacated by the pulling onside guard. His goal is to be quick enough to avoid contact with the center. When the center does get a piece of him, it may delay the nose tackle enough to be picked up by the inside block of the onside offensive tackle.

The offside end slants into the area vacated by the pulling offside guard. He looks for the fullback trying to seal the offside center-guard gap. He goes through the head of the fullback and often is in position to make a Big Play.

The onside end slants directly into the inside block of the tight end or tight slot, or the pin block by the setback. His momentum takes him to the block and puts him in an excellent position to fight through the head of the blocker.

The offside outside linebacker blitzes and checks the quarterback for the Waggle. He is responsible for outside contain. He is coached to get his hands on the quarterback to make him aware a defender is assigned to him.

The onside outside linebacker slants onside and goes through the head of a wing in a tight end-wing flank. Versus a flank with no wing, he slants to an imaginary man and keeps outside leverage on the play. He takes the pulling guard on with his inside flipper and is extremely careful not to get depth into the backfield. He plays on the line of scrimmage and does not give ground.

Normally, the secondary employs Roll coverage and executes it in the direction opposite the Slant. After taking their recognition steps, the defensive backs adjust to defend the run opposite their secondary call. (Diagrams 4-1, 4-2, 4-3 and 4-4)

DIAGRAM 4-1

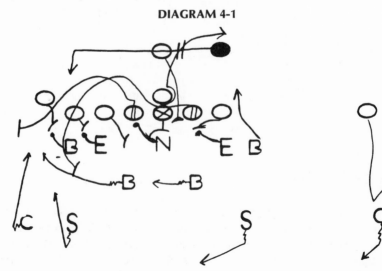

DIAGRAM 4-2

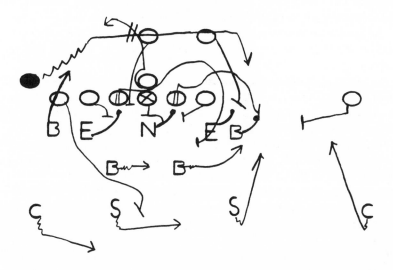

DIAGRAM 4-3

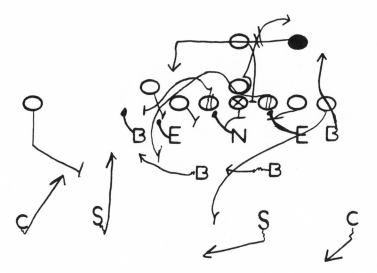

Using the Read Blitz

When the offensive guards pull, both inside linebackers blitz. The offside inside linebacker executes his blitz as near to the offside center-guard gap as possible. This takes him away from the offside offensive tackle who attempts to cut him off. As he executes the blitz, he eyeballs the fullback to make

DIAGRAM 4-4

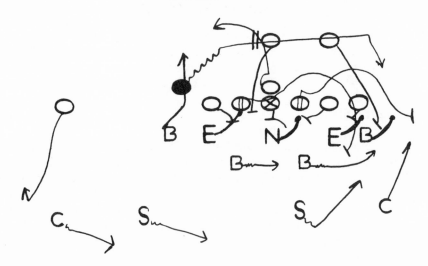

sure he does not have the ball. Once he is sure the fullback does not have the ball, he gets on a collision course with the ballcarrier.

The onside inside linebacker executes his blitz as near to the onside center-guard gap as possible. This takes him away from the onside offensive tackle who attempts to execute a down block on him. Going to his target point puts him in a good position to tackle the halfback for a big loss.

The nose tackle and ends execute their normal 3-4 reads and fight through pressure to the ball. All three are particularly careful to prohibit the offensive linemen, on whom they are aligned, from getting a block on the inside linebackers.

The outside linebackers execute their blitz. Unlike Slant, the offside linebacker is not responsible for outside contain. However, he still must check the quarterback for Waggle before pursuing the ball.

The secondary employs He-Man coverage. After making sure it is definitely a running play, they react to run. (Diagram 4-5)

DIAGRAM 4-5

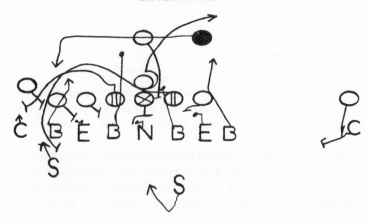

THE FULLBACK TRAP FROM
VARIOUS FORMATIONS

The Fullback Trap is another facet of the Sweep Series. As part of that series, it has the same formation tendencies as the Sweep and is run to the same side as the Sweep fake. The Fullback Dive may be run with blocking schemes other than trap. Gut or on blocking schemes may also be employed.

Using the Slant

The onside offensive guard blocks inside on the nose tackle. The onside inside linebacker steps up and slightly outside. He sees the onside offensive tackle out of the corner of his eye and steps to him to prevent being collapsed by an inside block.

The offside inside linebacker reads the pull of the offside offensive guard and steps in that direction. He reads the handoff to the fullback and slides parallel to the line of scrimmage with his movement. He is in an excellent position to make the play.

The nose tackle slants into the down block of the onside guard. He cannot allow himself to be pushed off the line of scrimmage by either the guard or the center-guard double-team. He fights through the face of the guard.

The offside end slants into the area vacated by the trapping guard. He, most often, is the defender who makes the play on the Trap. By getting in the "hip pocket" of the guard, he is on a straight line for a collision with the fullback.

The onside end executes his slant and is careful not to allow the tight end or tight slot an inside release on the linebacker.

Both outside linebackers execute their techniques and only become involved with the play as they pursue the ball. The onside linebacker remains conscious of the Sweep and the offside linebacker checks for Waggle.

The secondary, employing Roll coverage opposite the Slant, reads run and reacts to it. The safety, to the side of the play, should be the first defensive back to get to the ball. (Diagram 4-6)

Using the Read Blitz

The Fullback Trap is extremely difficult to run against the Read Blitz. Using a basic trap blocking scheme, the offside offensive tackle must prevent penetration by the offside inside linebacker. This is an extremely difficult task.

The best possible alternative for the offensive coach, who wants to remain in a trap blocking scheme, is to trap with the center blocking offside. This gives the center the job of blocking the offside inside linebacker with the help of the offside offensive tackle. This scheme can be effective versus the

DIAGRAM 4-6

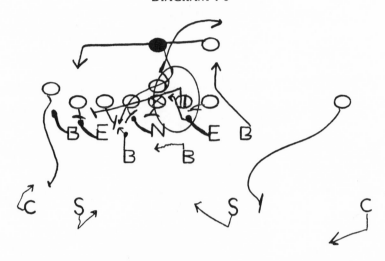

Read Blitz when the center is quick enough to prevent penetration by the offside linebacker. This scheme also forces the offside guard to single block the nose tackle. (Diagram 4-7)

DIAGRAM 4-7

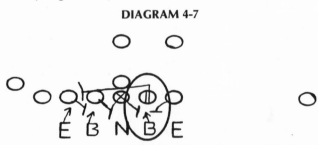

The many problems created by the use of "Fake Read Blitz" are apparent when alternative blocking schemes are devised to block Read Blitz. For the most part, schemes developed to handle the Read Blitz are less effective against the basic 3-4. The Fake Read Blitz, when the ball is snapped, is nothing more than our basic 3-4 defense.

Versus the Fake Read Blitz, the alternative trap blocking scheme is much less effective than the basic scheme. The center, who is responsible for the offside linebacker, has a great deal of trouble getting to him as he drops from his Up alignment on the snap of the ball. He no longer has a simple offside blocking angle. The onside guard still single blocks the nose tackle when the double-team would have been much more effective. (Diagram 4-8)

The offensive coach must decide to use basic blocking schemes or develop alternatives. Either way, the Read Blitz and Fake Read Blitz cause offensive dilemmas. These dilemmas create a definite advantage for the defense.

When the offense employs the basic trap blocking scheme, the onside guard blocks inside on the nose tackle. The onside inside linebacker jams

DIAGRAM 4-8

the guard and steps inside with him, attempting to keep him off the nose tackle. However, he does not go inside beyond the original alignment of his offside foot. He immediately feels for a down block by the onside tackle. When the down block occurs, he steps into the neck of the tackle and fights through his head.

The offside linebacker reads the pull of the offside guard and executes his blitz. He is in the best position to tackle the fullback for no gain.

The nose tackle fights the pressure of the double-team and the ends execute their normal 3-4 reads. The ends are particularly careful not to penetrate and become susceptible to the trap.

The outside linebackers execute their blitz. They check their responsibilities and then pursue the ball.

The secondary, employing He-Man coverage, makes sure it is a run before going to the ball. Since the fullback would be number two if it were a pass, the safety, to the offside, should be the first secondary defender to the ball. (Diagram 4-9)

DIAGRAM 4-9

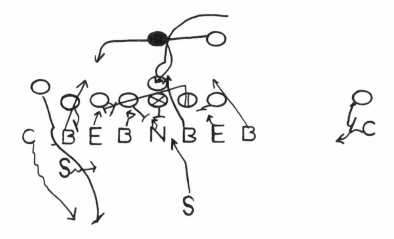

Chapter 5

Defending Against the FB Belly and HB Counter

The initial backfield action of the FB Belly is the starting point for many other Wing-T plays. The Belly Option (Chapter 6) and the Belly-Keep Pass (Chapter 8) are plays that continue outside flow after the Belly fake. For the Belly Option, the Belly fake is designed to delay defenders inside and give the offense a better opportunity to attack the flow-side flank. For the Belly-Keep Pass, the fake is used to encourage the linebackers and defensive backs to react to run and open up the passing lanes.

The HB Counter and Belly-Waggle Pass go opposite the flow action of the Belly. Both plays are designed to take advantage of a defense moving too quickly to defend the FB Belly.

THE FB BELLY FROM VARIOUS FORMATIONS

The Wing-T Offense employs several different methods of running the FB Belly, using various blocking schemes. The Slant and Read Blitz are effective against all of them. However, to describe defensing all methods of running the FB Belly would take much more space than allotted for one play in this text. To solve this problem, the most common method of running the FB Belly is described in this chapter. It involves a lead block by the setback and short motion by the other halfback, initially aligned as a wing or slot.

Both a cross blocking and an on blocking scheme are employed when using this method. For simplicity, the on blocking scheme is used in this description.

The FB Belly can be, and often is, executed effectively without any kind of motion by the offside halfback. However, the use of motion puts the offside halfback in the correct position to be the pitchman on the Belly Option or an effective log blocker on the Belly-Keep Pass. The FB Belly is another excellent example of the Series approach to offense used by the Wing-T. The defense is forced to stop the Belly, while having to be prepared to halt both companion plays.

The use of motion also gives the illusion the play will go in the direction of the motion. This helps set up the HB Counter and the Belly-Waggle Pass.

Using the Slant

When employing the on blocking scheme, the onside linebacker reads the inside block of the onside offensive guard and reacts to it. He uses the same initial steps he employed versus the FB Trap. Stepping up and slightly outside helps eliminate a log block by the pulling offside guard. He feels for a down block by the onside tackle as he looks into the backfield for the movement of his near back key. As he sees the movement of the fullback, he also sees the movement of the setback.

As the offensive tackle is blocking the slanting end outside, the setback takes his onside step outside and reads the block of the tackle. Since the tackle is blocking outside, the setback executes a lead block inside the block of the offensive tackle. Ideally, the halfback wants to pin the linebacker inside and have the fullback run outside his block and inside the block of the tackle.

The linebacker reads the movement of the setback and steps up to meet him. When the head of the blocker goes outside of him, he fights through his head to protect the onside guard-tackle gap. He keeps his hands on the blocker and his shoulders parallel to the line of scrimmage. This allows him to step inside or outside, depending on the movement of the fullback.

The offside linebacker reads the pull of the offside offensive guard and steps in that direction. He reads his near back key and makes sure he beats any attempt by the offside guard to pin him inside.

The nose tackle reacts to the inside block by the onside guard in the same manner that he reacted versus FB Trap. By fighting through the head of the guard, he compresses the onside center-guard gap and forces any cutback attempt to go behind the center-guard double-team into the "waiting arms" of the offside end.

The offside end slants into the area vacated by the pulling guard. As on FB Trap, the offside offensive tackle is responsible for preventing penetration by this defender, and this is an extremely difficult task. At worst, the offside end prevents any successful cutback play inside.

The onside end executes his slant and fights back through the pressure of the onside tackle's block. He attempts to push the tackle back into the guard-tackle gap, while keeping outside leverage on the ball. Keeping outside leverage is no problem; pushing the offensive tackle back into the guard-tackle gap is a difficult job.

The onside outside linebacker slants and is responsible for the pitch on Belly Option or the curl-to-flat on Belly-Keep Pass. Once he is sure neither of these plays is being run, he pursues the ball.

The offside outside linebacker blitzes and makes sure he is in position for any outside cutback. Once the threat of cutback or reverse disappears, he pursues the ball.

The secondary checks for a quarterback passing action opposite flow (Belly Waggle), then adjusts to defend the run. (Diagram 5-1)

DIAGRAM 5-1

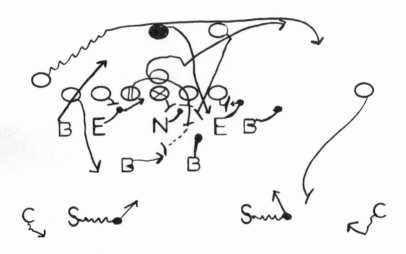

Using the Read Blitz

The Read Blitz creates the same problems for the FB Belly that it did for the FB Trap. By pulling the offside guard, the offensive tackle is left to stop the blitzing offside inside linebacker, a difficult task. The only way to eliminate this problem is to keep the offside guard "home."

Keeping the offside guard home is the most practical blocking scheme to employ. However, it forces one-on-one blocking along the line of scrimmage, a blocking variation not particularly popular with Wing-T enthusiasts. This blocking scheme, along with the setback as an extra blocker at the point of attack, is not a bad blocking scheme versus the Read Blitz and could cause this defensive scheme some trouble. The extra blocker at the point of attack could create a defensive problem. (Diagram 5-2) However, the offense does not get a steady diet of Read Blitz. Fake Read Blitz causes the offense a problem when the offside guard stays home. His job is to prevent the offside linebacker from flowing onside. Blocking the linebacker in this defensive scheme is much more difficult than blocking him when Read Blitz is used. (Diagram 5-3)

DIAGRAM 5-2

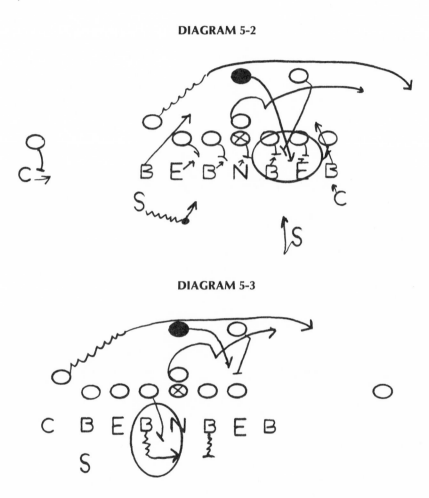

DIAGRAM 5-3

The offense also faces Slant and other facets of the 3-4 defensive package. The Slant, as well as other parts of the 3-4 scheme, can be executed from a Fake Read Blitz alignment. This further confuses the offense and helps eliminate the use of specific blocking schemes designed to combat the Read Blitz.

When the basic blocking scheme is employed, the nose tackle, onside inside linebacker, and both ends react to their normal 3-4 reads.

The offside inside linebacker reads the pull of the offside guard and executes his blitz. As in FB Trap, he is in an excellent position to make the play.

The outside linebackers execute their blitz. The onside linebacker makes sure the quarterback does not have the ball on Belly Option or Belly-Keep Pass before he pursues the ball. The offside linebacker checks for cutback or reverse before he gets into his proper angle of pursuit.

The defensive backs, using He-Man coverage, make sure all threats of pass are gone before they react to the ball. Since there is no number two releasing to his side, the offside safety is the first secondary defender to the ball. (Diagram 5-4)

DIAGRAM 5-4

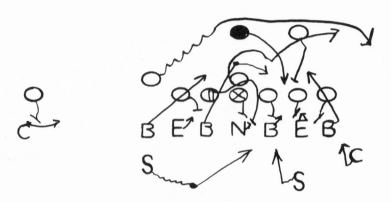

THE HB COUNTER FROM
VARIOUS FORMATIONS

The HB Counter helps the Wing-T Offense, and hinders the defense of opponents, in two significant ways. First, the play takes advantage of a defense whose offside defenders overreact to a flow play like the FB Belly. Second, the mere threat of the counter play forces offside defenders to pursue flow plays too slowly and gives the offense a distinct advantage. The Slant and Read Blitz neutralize these two defensive advantages.

Using the Slant

For the onside inside linebacker, his initial line read is the same as FB Trap. He steps up and slightly outside and fights through the head of the onside tackle, who attempts to pin him inside. He looks to the fullback as his near back key. As the fullback flows away, the linebacker picks up the counter action of the offside setback and reads ball.

The offside inside linebacker reads the first movement of the offside guard. However, this guard is pushed off his path to the linebacker by the slanting nose tackle. The linebacker then checks his backfield key. As he sees Belly action, he sees the counter movement of the setback and the offside tackle pulling across the ball. He reacts to both.

With the nose tackle slanting away from the onside guard, the guard continues to the next level and tries to block the offside linebacker. Once the linebacker sees the counter movement of the setback and the offside pulling tackle, he flows onside, expecting to meet the onside guard. He attacks the blocker and fights through his head to the ball.

The nose tackle slants to the offside guard and knocks him off his path to the linebacker. He fights through the pressure of the center's block and works his way to the ball. As he keeps his shoulders parallel to the line of scrimmage, he protects against cutback.

The onside end slants directly into the trapping offside tackle and forces him into the onside center-guard gap. He keeps outside leverage on the ball and forces the running back to spill outside.

The offside end slants and checks for the quarterback running the Counter Bootleg Pass. Once he is sure the ball was handed off, he pursues the play.

The onside outside linebacker executes his blitz. He is in an excellent position to pick up the ballcarrier as he spills outside.

The offside outside linebacker checks for Counter Bootleg Pass and then pursues the ball.

The secondary, in Roll coverage to the side of the play, reads and reacts to run. The safeties are the first secondary defenders to the ball. (Diagram 5-5)

DIAGRAM 5-5

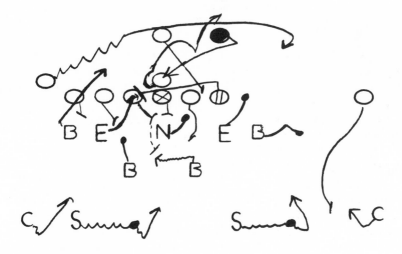

Using the Read Blitz

The key to stopping the HB Counter is the play of the onside inside linebacker and the onside end.

The onside inside linebacker plays the inside block of the onside guard like FB Trap. He jams the guard but does not go too far inside with him and allow the offensive tackle a successful down block. He steps into the neck of the onside tackle and fights through his head to the ball.

The offside inside linebacker reads the head of the offside guard and fights through his face to the ball.

The nose tackle reacts to the pressure of the double-team and does not allow himself to be pushed off the line of scrimmage. The least expected of him is a stalemate.

The onside end attacks the attempted down block by the onside tackle. He fights to keep him off the linebacker. He is very careful not to penetrate and become susceptible to the Trap. He attacks the trapper and forces the ballcarrier to spill outside.

The offside end gets into the "hip pocket" of the pulling tackle and looks for the fullback. He does not allow the fullback to cut him off from the ball. He goes through the head of the fullback and continues along the line of scrimmage.

Both outside linebackers perform their blitz. The onside linebacker looks for the ballcarrier spilling outside. The offside linebacker checks the quarterback for Counter Bootleg Pass.

In He-Man coverage, the secondary reads and reacts to run. The onside safety is the first defensive back to the ball since the ballcarrier is number two to his side. (Diagram 5-6)

DIAGRAM 5-6

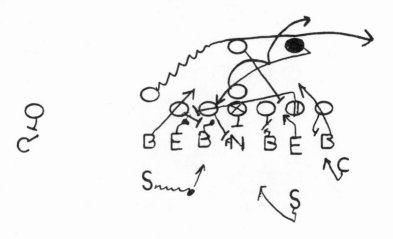

Chapter 6

Defending Against
the Belly Option
and Sprint Option

One important aspect of the Wing-T Offense is the ability to attack one area in several different ways. As far as the inside running game is concerned, the FB Trap and the HB Counter Draw are two excellent examples of this ability.

To achieve consistent success with the FB Trap (Chapter 4), all defenders must be blocked at the point of attack. However, this is not true of the HB Counter Draw. This play, while attacking the same area as FB Trap, makes use of finesse and deception at the point of attack. Rather than being blocked, the defensive end is finessed out of the play by a fake pass block. (Diagram 6-1)

DIAGRAM 6-1

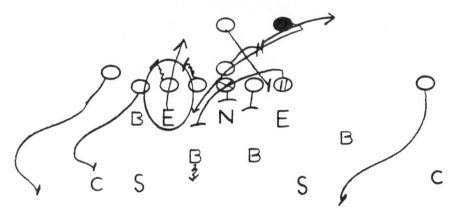

When attacking the outside, or flank, the Wing-T also makes use of power and finesse plays. The Buck Sweep (Chapter 4) and the Lead Sweep use power as a means of advancing the ball. The Belly Option, Sprint Option, and Trap Option all use finesse.

Due to the limits placed on space in this text, this chapter deals only with the Belly Option and Sprint Option.

THE BELLY OPTION FROM
VARIOUS FORMATIONS

The Belly Option is another facet of the Belly Series. Its success is dependent upon the ability of the quarterback-fullback fake to momentarily freeze inside defenders and allow the offense a numerical advantage at the point of attack.

The Belly Option is not a Triple Option, but the defense is required to defend it as such. When the ball is faked to the fullback, the defense does not know if the play is FB Belly or Belly Option. As a result, the defense has to be prepared to stop the fullback as well as the quarterback and pitchman (offside halfback).

Naturally, the Belly Option is run from the same formations as the FB Belly. However, with the Belly Option, motion is always employed. This is necessary to get the offside HB, who becomes the pitchman, in the proper relationship with the quarterback. Either short or two-step motion is used. (Diagrams 6-2, 6-3)

DIAGRAM 6-2

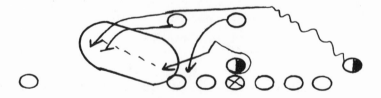

DIAGRAM 6-3

Using the Slant

Both inside linebackers read the initial onside movements of the offensive guards on whom they are aligned. Both guards are bumped off their paths to the linebackers by slanting defensive linemen (offside end and nose tackle). As both linebackers check their backfield key, and see no counter action by either halfback, they begin to move with the flow.

The onside linebacker makes sure there is no handoff to the fullback before moving to the flank. He is also aware of the onside offensive tackle who may miss his block on the onside slanting end and go to the next level to block the linebacker.

The three down defensive linemen slant onside and attempt to avoid the blocks of the offensive players on whom they were originally aligned. Once the offside end and nose tackle reach their target points, they pursue the play.

Once the onside end realizes it is the Belly Option, he steps back off the line of scrimmage and plays the ball from this position. Being off the line of scrimmage allows the end a better chance of attacking the quarterback if he turns up inside. It also allows him a better angle on the pitchman when the quarterback pitches the ball. (Diagram 6-4)

DIAGRAM 6-4

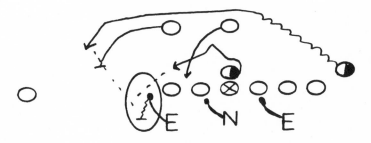

The onside outside linebacker slants and plays the lead blocker on the line of scrimmage. He attacks the blocker and forces him inside. The linebacker keeps his shoulders parallel to the line and keeps outside leverage on the ball. While keeping outside leverage, the linebacker *never* gives ground. Giving ground can create a running lane for the pitchman and makes the job of the alley defender more difficult.

The offside outside linebacker looks for Reverse or Belly Bootleg Pass before he pursues the ball.

The secondary recognizes run and moves to the ball. The onside safety becomes an extra defender to the side of the play while the other safety becomes the alley defender. Both safeties attack the ball after it crosses the line of scrimmage. (Diagram 6-5)

DIAGRAM 6-5

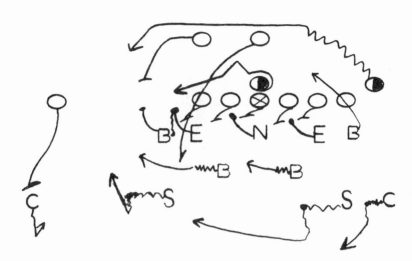

Using the Read Blitz

The inside linebackers, nose tackle, and ends play through the head of the players on whom they initially align. They play on the line of scrimmage and do not allow themselves to be pushed off the line. This helps eliminate an onside crease into which the quarterback could run.

The onside outside linebacker fires directly into the face of the quarterback, forcing a fast pitch.

When Slant is employed and the Option is executed to the side of the Slant, the quarterback is played with a "soft" technique. This is also true of other parts of the 3-4 package. The various methods of playing the quarterback keep him off balance and do not give him the luxury of developing a definite pattern for when to pitch the ball.

The offside outside linebacker checks for Reverse and Belly Bootleg Pass before pursuing the play.

Playing the various Options with man-to-man coverage can cause serious defensive problems. However, He-Man coverage eliminates these problems. Since the safety is responsible for number two to his side, he is in an excellent position to play the pitch. The lead blocker is number two and the safety does not allow himself to be pinned inside by the blocker.

Because there is no number two to his side, the offside safety becomes a free safety. As the free safety, he is the alley defender to the side of the Option. (Diagram 6-6)

THE SPRINT OPTION FROM VARIOUS FORMATIONS

Unlike the other Option Plays in the Wing-T Offense, the Sprint Option has no inside fake to hold defenders. The play takes advantage of a defense

DIAGRAM 6-6

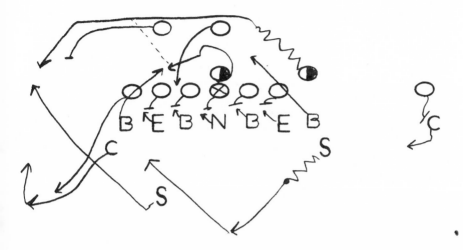

whose pre-snap alignment or post-snap, predetermined movements give the offense a possible numerical advantage at the point of attack.

Using the Slant

The Sprint Option attacks the flank opposite the normal direction of the Slant. This, to some Wing-T opponents, may appear to be an offensive advantage. It certainly is not.

Both inside linebackers read the initial movement of the offensive guards on whom they are aligned. However, both guards are knocked off their paths to the linebacker by the slanting defensive linemen. The linebackers then focus their attention on their near back key and move toward the onside.

The three down defensive linemen slant away from the play. Upon reaching their target points, they react to the play and get into the proper angle of pursuit. The offside end makes sure all threats of Reverse are gone before pursuing the play.

The onside outside linebacker blitzes into the face of the quarterback and forces a fast pitch. He is particularly mindful of making the quarterback "pay the price" for attempting to carry the ball. A few great hits on the quarterback create the possibility of premature pitches later in the game.

The offside end executes his slant and looks for a Reverse or Throwback Pass before pursuing the play.

The secondary, using Roll coverage opposite the direction of the Slant, is in a great position to defend against the play.

When Cup is called, the onside corner rotates up to defend against the pitch. He does not cross the line of scrimmage and does not allow the lead blocker to kick him out. He keeps outside leverage on the ball as he forces the blocker inside. He fights to keep his shoulders parallel to the line of scrimmage. He cannot give ground and cannot be knocked down by a block below the knees. (Diagram 6-7)

When Ivy is called, the onside safety defends against the pitch. Like the corner with Cup, he does not cross the line of scrimmage, and he does not give ground. He does not allow the lead blocker to pin him inside; he fights through the blocker and keeps outside leverage on the ball. He cannot be knocked down by a low block.

The offside safety, in both Cup and Ivy, becomes the alley defender after checking the deep middle one-third zone for a pass. (Diagram 6-8)

DIAGRAM 6-7

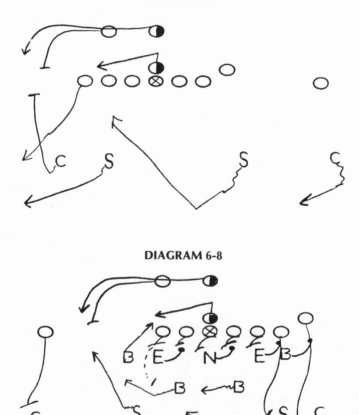

DIAGRAM 6-8

Using the Read Blitz

The inside linebackers, nose tackle, and ends fight through the attempted reach blocks of the players on whom they are originally aligned. The defenders are always mindful of going through the head of the blockers and never going "backdoor" on a block. (Diagram 6-9)

DIAGRAM 6-9

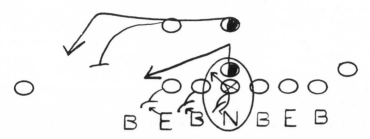

The onside outside linebacker executes his blitz and is quickly in the face of the quarterback. As previously described, he forces a fast pitch.

He-Man coverage allows the onside safety to cover number two; this puts him in a very good position to defend against the pitch. He plays the Sprint Option in the same manner that he played the Belly Option.

Unlike most Wing-T Options, the Sprint Option has a number two releasing on both the onside and offside. Therefore, there is no free safety to act as an alley defender to the onside. He-Man coverage becomes pure man-to-man as the offside safety covers the offside number two. This does present a defensive problem.

This problem is partially solved by the lack of an offensive inside fake. This allows the front defenders, particularly those on the onside, the freedom to get to the onside flank quickly. This onside movement, together with the correct pursuit angles by the offside defenders, prevents a cutback by the quarterback.

The corners stay with their men until the ball crosses the line of scrimmage. Once the ball crosses the line, they pursue the play. (Diagram 6-10)

DIAGRAM 6-10

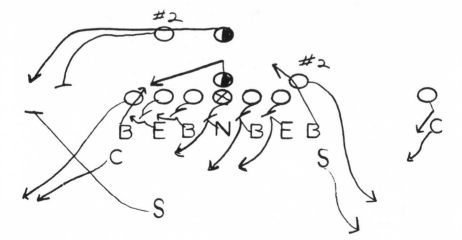

Chapter 7

Defending Against the Waggle Pass

The Waggle Pass is the best known Wing-T Play-Action Pass. This one play presents the possibility of a run to both flanks and up the middle while posing the threat of a pass to all three deep zones, the middle hook area, and both flats. (Diagram 7-1)

DIAGRAM 7-1

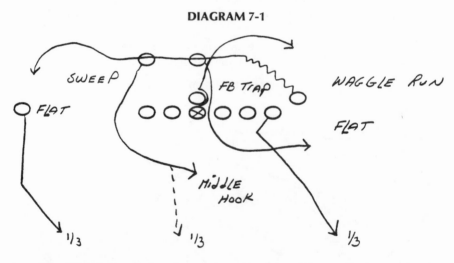

The Waggle is designed to take advantage of two possible defensive errors. When the defensive coach does not assign a defender to contain the quarterback, away from the Sweep action, the quarterback is free to attack the onside flank. When the quarterback attacks the flank, he puts the defender, responsible for the onside flat area, in a serious bind. If the defender comes up to stop the quarterback, the flat area is left open and the fullback is free to catch a pass for a significant gain. If the defender remains in the flat area, the quarterback is free to run the ball for a significant gain. (Diagrams 7-2, 7-3)

DIAGRAM 7-2

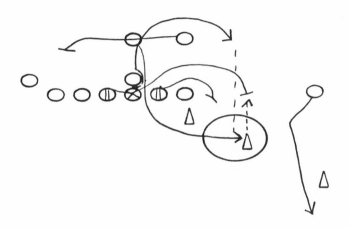

DIAGRAM 7-3

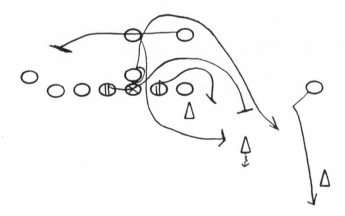

The second possible error occurs when any member of the secondary, or either inside linebacker, overreacts to either run fake (Fullback Trap or Sweep). This takes him out of position, and he cannot successfully defend against a pass pattern in his zone coverage area.

The Slant and Read Blitz help eliminate the possibility of either error.

THE WAGGLE PASS FROM
VARIOUS FORMATIONS

The Waggle Pass is executed toward a setback or the wing or slot, using short motion to carry out the Sweep fake. Therefore, the Waggle Pass is run toward a single receiver flank, either a tight end or a split end.

For simplicity, this chapter employs only two formations in analyzing the Waggle Pass - a wing formation with no motion and a wing formation with wing short motion.

Using the Slant

The onside inside linebacker reads the outside pull of the onside guard. He takes one step with the guard and reads his near back key, the fullback. The linebacker steps up and collisions the fullback before going to his zone coverage area. If the ball is given to the fullback on a Sucker play, the linebacker is there to stop it. When the fullback is running a pattern to the flat area, the collision delays the pattern and gives the defender responsible for that area extra time to react to pass.

Upon recognition of Waggle Pass, the onside linebacker goes to the onside curl area versus a split end. Versus a tight end, he goes to the onside hook area. He checks for any onside pattern in his area before looking for offside number two, running a drag pattern. He does not come up to cover the fullback. If offside number two does not get as far as the onside linebacker's area of responsibility, he continues to cushion back.

The offside inside linebacker reads the inside pull of the offside guard. He also reads the fullback as his near back key. When he recognizes Waggle Pass, he looks for offside number two as he drops into the hole. He attempts to collision offside number two and make him "pay the price" for running a drag pattern through the middle hook area.

The nose tackle slants offside to the area vacated by the offside guard. As soon as he sees the guard pulling inside, he realizes he must fight through the center's block to get to the onside. He goes through the head of the center and not backdoor.

The onside end reacts in much the same manner as the nose tackle. He slants to the onside guard who is pulling outside. He fights through the head of the onside tackle and, like the nose tackle, does not go backdoor.

The offside end slants and attempts to collision the halfback who is making the Sweep fake. This collision may force the back to block the end and not release into the flat as a possible number three receiver to the offside.

The onside outside linebacker blitzes and is the defender who has the responsibility of keeping the quarterback inside and not allowing him to attack the flank. In other words, the linebacker has contain responsibility. This defender often beats the attempted block by the onside guard and tackles the quarterback for a considerable loss.

To give the offense a different look, the inside and outside linebackers, away from the Slant, execute a Switch. On Waggle action, the linebackers exchange responsibilities. When the inside linebacker reads the outside pull of the onside guard and sees Waggle Pass, he blitzes outside the onside offensive tackle and contains the quarterback. The onside outside linebacker, upon recognition of Waggle Pass, drops into the curl area and assumes the normal pass responsibilities of the onside inside linebacker.

This stunt tends to give the quarterback the idea he can successfully attack the flank. Neither the quarterback nor either guard expects contain responsibility from an inside linebacker. This stunt leads to some great hits on the unsuspecting quarterback. (Diagram 7-4)

The offside outside linebacker slants and, upon recognition of Waggle Pass, executes his comeback technique. If the halfback, faking Sweep, gets to the offside flat, the linebacker picks him up man-to-man. This technique is also helpful versus the Waggle Screen Pass. It puts the linebacker in a good position to stop the play. (Diagram 7-5)

DIAGRAM 7-4

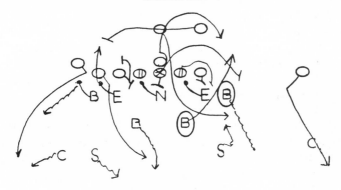

DIAGRAM 7-5

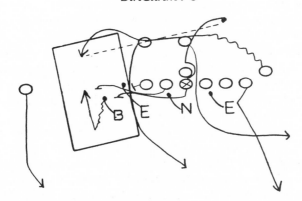

The secondary, in Roll coverage, rotates to the side of the Waggle Pass. Depending on the split of the offside end, either Cup or Ivy is employed.

When Cup is employed, the onside corner levels to cover the flat area. He picks up the fullback in the onside flat. The onside safety rotates into the deep outside one-third zone and picks up the end running the Waggle pattern. (Diagram 7-6)

DIAGRAM 7-6

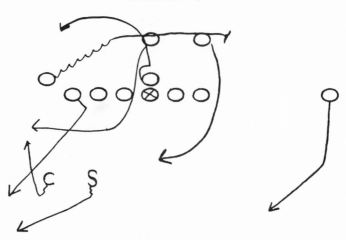

When Ivy is employed, the onside corner and onside safety exchange responsibilities.

With both Cup and Ivy, the offside safety is responsible for the deep middle one-third zone. He covers the deepest receiver in his zone. The deepest receiver may be offside number one, running a post pattern, or offside number two, running a deep drag pattern.

When offside number two runs the drag pattern, he reads the offside safety. When the safety drops to cover the post pattern by offside number one, offside number two attempts to get in the area between the offside linebacker, covering the hole, and the safety. The offside inside linebacker reads the pattern of offside number two and drops with him, forcing the quarterback to throw over him to get the ball to number two.

The offside corner drops into the offside deep outside one-third zone. Since there is no other threat to his zone, he uses man-to-man coverage versus the post pattern by offside number one. He communicates this to the offside safety. Upon hearing the call from the offside corner, the offside safety can stay back and help with the post pattern or come up and help with offside number two, if he gets too far behind the offside inside linebacker.

Some Wing-T teams run the offside number one on a fly pattern rather than a post pattern. This is much better for the defense as it allows the offside safety to cover a deep drag by offside number two and takes considerable pressure off the offside inside linebacker. (Diagram 7-7)

DIAGRAM 7-7

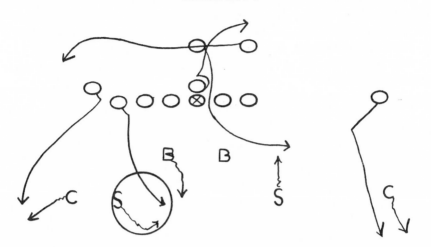

The Slant is an excellent defense versus the Waggle Pass and adequately covers all facets of the play. (Diagram 7-8)

DIAGRAM 7-8

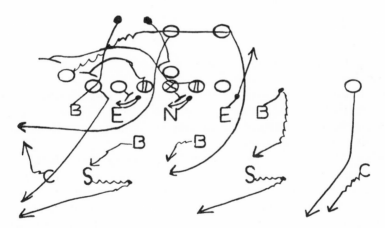

Using the Read Blitz

We believe the Read Blitz is the best possible defense versus the Waggle Pass. There are several reasons for this belief. If the offense attempts to release four receivers, as is often the case, there are not enough blockers remaining to pick up the seven rushers. Since the onside outside linebacker forces the quarterback to pull up prematurely, it does not matter from what point along the line of scrimmage the unblocked rusher comes. By his original alignment, the unblocked rusher is always close enough to the quarterback to get a sack or, at least, a hurry.

When the offense releases only three receivers and the fullback remains as a blocker, the offense is forced to block every rusher one-on-one. We believe this is an advantage for the defense. However, the quarterback does get a bit more time to pass when the offense is capable of putting one blocker on every rusher. The Read Blitz automatically compensates for the quarterback's additional time by having a free pass defender, the free safety, in center field.

The onside inside linebacker blitzes behind the pull of the onside guard. He blitzes to his target point. Since the first job of the fullback is to protect the area vacated by the onside guard, he tries to block the onside linebacker. However, the linebacker goes to a point two yards wider than the original alignment of the fullback and his target point is much more onside than the path the fullback takes to fake Fullback Trap. To prevent the linebacker from sacking the quarterback, the fullback must get his head to the onside of the linebacker and block him outside-in. Because of the linebacker's target point and angle of attack, this is an extremely tough job. When the fullback blocks the linebacker inside-out, he cannot prevent him from getting to the quarterback. (Diagram 7-9)

DIAGRAM 7-9

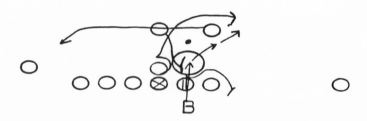

The offside inside linebacker executes his blitz. Since the center is blocking the nose tackle and the offside offensive tackle is blocking the offside end, the only blocker who can possibly block him is the offside guard. The guard has to pull onside and turn back to the offside to pick him up. This is a very difficult block and gives the offside linebacker a good opportunity to get a sack.

The nose tackle and both ends fight through the heads of their blockers and rush the passer. The onside end is very careful to keep outside leverage on the onside tackle as he has contain responsibility on the quarterback.

The onside outside linebacker employs his blitz technique. Since he does not have contain responsibility, he can be very reckless with his rush.

The offside outside linebacker blitzes and the halfback, faking the Sweep, blocks him. When the halfback avoids the block and releases into the flat, the outside linebacker has him man-to-man. When the halfback does release into the flat, he becomes number three to the offside and the only defender in a good position to cover him is the offside outside linebacker.

Each corner picks up number one to his side and covers him man-to-man.

Both safeties cover number two to their side. When the fullback stays in to block the onside linebacker, the onside safety becomes free and goes to the ball when thrown. (Diagram 7-10)

DIAGRAM 7-10

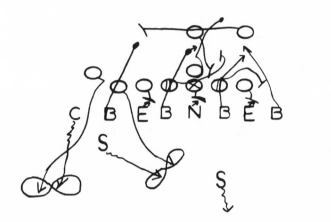

Chapter 8

Defending Against
the Belly Pass
and Sweep Pass

Even though the Wing-T makes use of other passing actions, Play-Action Passes make up the bulk of the passing offense. These Play-Action Passes fall into three categories. The Waggle Pass (Chapter 7) is an example of a Counter-Action Pass, the Belly Pass is a Flow-Action Pass, and the Sweep Pass is a combination of both.

THE BELLY PASS FROM
VARIOUS FORMATIONS

When employing the Belly Pass, the quarterback fakes the Fullback Belly and continues his passing action to the side of the flow. As in the Waggle Pass, the fake of the fullback is very important. Without a good fake, the linebackers will not react to run, and this is critical for a successful play.

With both the Waggle Pass and the Belly Pass, the quarterback has the option of running the football when the defender, responsible for contain, is blocked to the inside. When running the Waggle Pass, this blocking assignment belongs to the onside guard. With Belly Pass, it is the job of the offside halfback. However, on both plays, if the assigned blocker cannot hook the defender, he attempts to kick him out. The quarterback, most often, sets up and passes at this point. (Diagram 8-1)

When executing the Belly Pass, the offside halfback employs motion, just as he did with Belly Option. When aligned as a setback, two-step motion

DIAGRAM 8-1

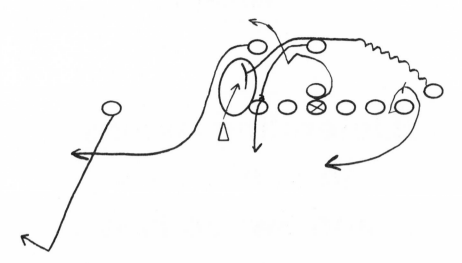

is employed. When originally aligned as either a slot or wing, short motion is used. The use of motion puts the offside halfback in a position to effectively block the defender responsible for contain. The use of motion also presents the possibility of Belly Option to the defense.

Since the play is part of the Belly Series, the defense cannot overreact to the possibility of either Fullback Belly or Belly Option. When they do, several problems occur, particularly when zone pass coverage is used.

When the onside inside linebacker bites on the Fullback Belly fake, the onside hook and curl areas become open. If onside number two runs an arc-and-up pattern or onside number one executes a curl, both are open. (Diagrams 8-2, 8-3)

DIAGRAM 8-2

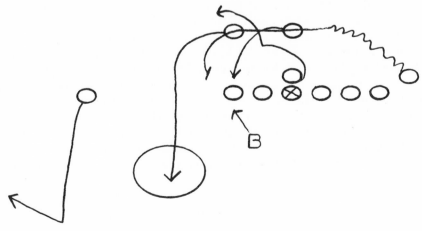

DIAGRAM 8-3

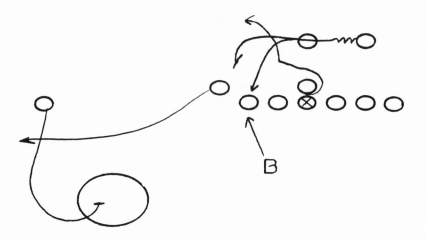

When the offside inside linebacker overreacts to the run fake, the middle hook or hole is open. If offside number one runs a drag pattern, he is open. (Diagram 8-4)

DIAGRAM 8-4

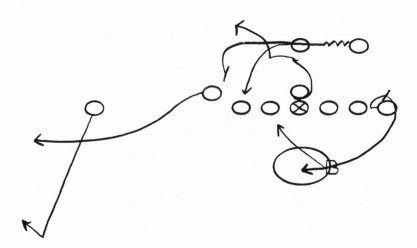

When the defender, responsible for contain, even slightly bites on the Fullback Belly fake, he becomes susceptible to the hook block by the offside halfback. When the block is effective, the quarterback is free to attack the flank. This is the same problem that occurs when the contain defender is blocked versus the Waggle Pass. The defender, responsible for the flat area, must either attack the quarterback and leave the receiver open, or stay in the flat area and give the quarterback room to run. (Diagram 8-5)

DIAGRAM 8-5

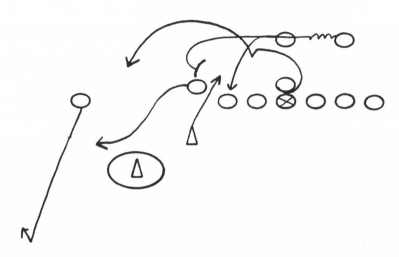

When the defender, responsible for the flat area, reacts up too quickly to defend against the possibility of the Belly Option, the onside number two becomes open. The overreacting defender is totally out of the play. He is too far from the quarterback to sack or hurry him and not close enough to number two to intercept the ball or knock it down. (Diagram 8-6)

DIAGRAM 8-6

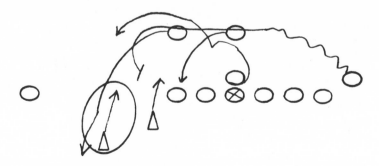

The Belly Pass is run from the same formations as the Belly Option. For simplicity, the formations used in the description of the Belly Option (Chapter 6) are employed in this chapter.

Using the Slant

The onside inside linebacker reads the area block of the onside guard. Since the guard does not come across the line of scrimmage to block him, the linebacker thinks pass and begins to drop into his pass responsibility area. As he drops, he eyeballs his near back key, the fullback, and moves with the backfield flow.

The offside inside linebacker reads the cup block by the offside guard. As he drops, he reads his near back key to determine flow and to make sure the onside halfback is not running the Halfback Counter with an onside pass blocking scheme. Once he is sure there is no counter action, he drops into the hole and looks for offside number one, running a drag pattern.

The nose tackle slants onside and attempts to beat the block of the center. When he executes a successful Slant, the onside guard helps the center, and a double-team is created. The nose tackle fights pressure and rushes the passer.

The onside end slants and becomes outside contain. He must beat the attempted block by the onside tackle and cannot allow himself to be pinned inside by the offside halfback.

The offside end executes his slant to the offside guard and reads his cup block. He rushes the passer by going through the head of the guard and not around his block.

The onside outside linebacker slants and determines if the play is Belly Option or Belly Pass. Once he recognizes pass, he drops to his area of pass responsibility.

The offside outside linebacker blitzes and rushes the passer. When he sees the quarterback flowing away, he flattens his path and rushes toward the upfield shoulder of the quarterback.

The secondary executes Roll opposite the direction of the Slant. The onside corner picks up the pattern of number one in the deep outside one-third zone. The onside safety goes to the deep middle zone and is aware of any deep drag pattern by offside number one.

The offside safety, covering the deep offside one-third zone, stays with the tight end since there is no other possible threat to his zone. We do not want him to just sit in the zone and cover grass.

When the offside corner sees no possibility of a receiver coming into his zone, he flows to the onside to help out. (Diagram 8-7)

Using the Read Blitz

The Read Blitz is a better defense, versus the Belly Pass, than the Slant. When Read Blitz is employed, the onside outside linebacker provides a fast outside pass rush. The rusher attacks quickly enough to get to the quarterback before the offside halfback has an opportunity to pin him inside.

He-Man coverage provides man-to-man coverage on all three receivers in the pattern. If the fullback drifts into the pattern, the free safety (offside

DIAGRAM 8-7

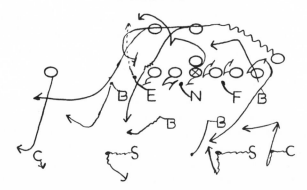

safety) can come up and take him. However, when four receivers release, there are not enough blockers to handle the seven rushers.

The inside linebackers get their hands on the guards to occupy their blocks. Since the guards do not pull, both linebackers drop to their zone pass responsibility areas.

The nose tackle and ends play through the heads of the players on whom they originally align and execute a good pass rush. The onside end is careful, once he beats the block of the onside tackle, not to get pinned inside by the offside halfback. He always keeps outside leverage and has contain responsibility.

The onside outside linebacker blitzes directly into the face of the quarterback. Since he is never expected to tackle the fullback on Fullback Belly, he does not bite on the Belly fake. This play looks like Belly Option and he attacks both plays in the same manner.

The offside outside linebacker executes his blitz and is normally unblocked. He looks for Reverse or Belly Bootleg as he flies to the quarterback. When the onside outside linebacker and the onside end force the quarterback to pull up, the offside outside linebacker has a good chance of getting a sack or a hurry. Some Wing-T teams, to eliminate this problem, keep the tight end home to pick up the offside outside linebacker.

Each corner picks up number one to his side and covers him man-to-man.

The onside safety covers number two to his side, while the offside safety becomes a free safety. If the fullback drifts out of the backfield and into the pattern, the free safety can pick him up. (Diagram 8-8)

THE SWEEP PASS FROM
VARIOUS FORMATIONS

The Sweep Pass is a combination Counter- and Flow-Action Pass. The Counter Action is provided by the fake of the Fullback Trap and the passing action of the quarterback, opposite the direction of the fake. When the

DIAGRAM 8-8

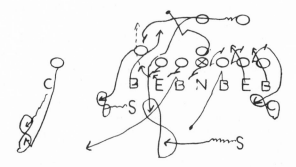

quarterback fakes Sweep to the offside halfback and continues his passing action to the same side as the fake, this is the Flow-Action phase of the play.

The Sweep Pass also features a flood-pass pattern to the onside. The flat area is attacked at two different levels. The wing, after faking an inside block to simulate Sweep, runs a deep flat pattern. The offside halfback, after faking Sweep, employs a flair pattern. This puts the defender responsible for the flat area in a bit of a bind.

This Play-Action Pass is an excellent play to run when the offense is having success with the Buck Sweep. The inside step by the tight end and wing can force an overreaction to the possibility of Sweep by the defenders responsible for the onside flat area and the onside deep outside one-third zone. This overreaction can leave the tight end or the wing open in the area they are attacking. (Diagram 8-9)

DIAGRAM 8-9

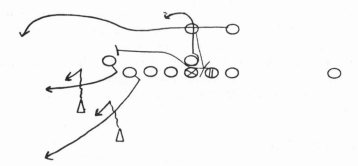

The Sweep Pass is part of the Buck Sweep Series and has the same formation requirements as the Buck Sweep (Chapter 4).

Using the Slant

The onside inside linebacker initially reacts as he did versus Belly Pass. Since the onside guard does not come across the line of scrimmage to block him, the linebacker thinks pass and begins to drop to his pass responsibility area. As he reads his near back key, the fullback, he makes sure he does not have the ball and then continues to drop.

The offside inside linebacker reads the inside pull of the offside guard. As he steps with the pull, he checks the fullback, his near back key, to be sure he does not have the ball on a Sucker Play. As he reads pass, he drops into the hole and looks for a drag pattern from offside number one.

The nose tackle executes his slant and attempts to beat the center's block. Since the onside guard has no defender to block, he turns back inside to help with the nose tackle. The nose tackle fights through the pressure and rushes the passer.

The onside end slants and becomes outside contain. He keeps outside leverage on the pulling guard and jams him, forcing the quarterback to pull up and not attack the flank. He cannot give ground to the pulling guard. Giving ground creates an inside running lane into which the quarterback can run.

The offside end slants into the area vacated by the offside guard. He looks for the fullback as he did with both Sweep and Fullback Trap (Chapter 4). As the fullback tries to block him, he goes through his head and rushes the passer.

The onside outside linebacker slants to the wing. He reads pass and drops into his pass area of responsibility. He covers the deepest receiver in his zone, the wing. When the ball is thrown to the offside halfback, running a flair pattern, he breaks on the ball and allows the receiver little or no gain.

The offside outside linebacker blitzes and makes sure no Counter Plays are coming his way before he rushes the passer. Since he is, at times, left unblocked, he has an excellent chance to record a sack or, at least, a hurry.

The secondary Rolls away from the Slant. The onside corner covers the tight end in the deep outside one-third zone.

The offside corner covers the deep outside one-third zone to the offside. When offside number one runs a deep drag, he stays with the pattern since there is little possibility of a receiver entering his area.

The onside safety covers the deep middle one-third zone and looks for a deep drag pattern from offside number one.

The offside safety, in Ivy rotation, executes his comeback technique and covers the drag pattern man-to-man. (Diagram 8-10)

Using the Read Blitz

The Sweep Pass, versus the Read Blitz, forces the onside outside linebacker to play onside number three man-to-man. He is the only defender in a position to effectively play this back. This puts additional pressure on the onside end. Since there is no fierce outside rush by the onside outside linebacker to force the quarterback to pull up, the onside end has to beat the block of the onside tackle and contain the quarterback. Contain is his normal responsibility in Read Blitz. Normally, however, the onside outside linebacker is exerting a very quick and hard outside blitz to aid the end's contain responsibility.

DIAGRAM 8-10

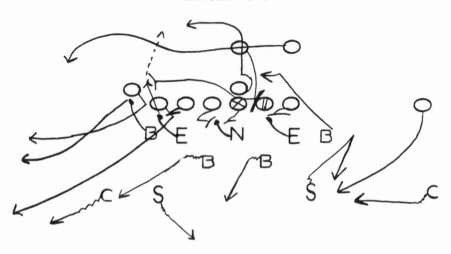

Since the onside offensive guard does not pull, the onside inside linebacker puts his hands on the guard to occupy his block. He then drops into the curl area.

The nose tackle and offside end fight through the heads of the blockers on whom they are aligned.

The offside inside linebacker executes his blitz behind the onside pull of the offside guard. He eyeballs the fullback to make sure he does not have the ball on a Sucker Play. When he is sure the fullback does not have the ball, he attempts to avoid his block. If the fullback does make contact with him, he fights through the fullback's head and sprints to the quarterback.

The onside end fights through the onside shoulder of the offensive tackle and contains the quarterback. When employing Slant, his initial slant move takes him outside and he does not have a difficult task beating the tackle's block. With Read Blitz, he fights through the tackle and this is a more difficult job. This, coupled with the lack of outside pressure by the onside outside linebacker, makes his contain responsibility even harder to accomplish. (Diagrams 8-11, 8-12).

Once the onside end achieves contain position, he attacks the pulling guard just as he does when Slant is employed. He forces the quarterback to pull up, giving the offside outside linebacker the opportunity to sack or hurry the passer.

The onside outside linebacker begins his blitz and sees number three running a pattern. He alters his path and picks him up man-to-man. This transition from a reckless rusher to a controlled pass defender is a difficult task and one to be practiced during the week.

The offside outside linebacker blitzes and looks for any counter action. When the onside end forces the quarterback to pull up, the offside outside linebacker has a chance for a sack or a hurry.

DIAGRAM 8-11

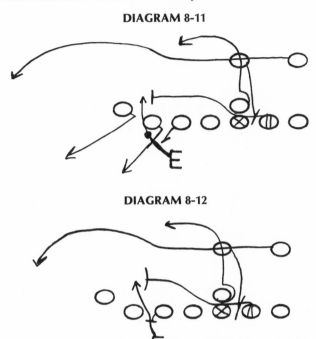

DIAGRAM 8-12

Each corner takes number one to his side and stays with him until the ball is thrown or until the quarterback crosses the line of scrimmage.

The onside safety takes number two man-to-man, while the offside safety becomes free. (Diagram 8-13)

DIAGRAM 8-13

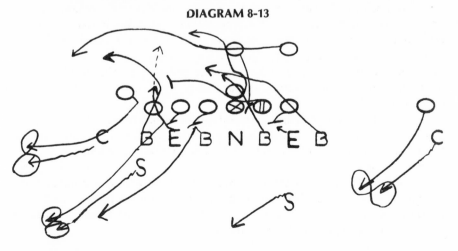

Chapter 9

Defending Against the Sprint-Out Pass

The Sprint-Out Pass is another important part of the Wing-T Passing Attack. The basic alignment of the fullback makes this type of passing action simple to employ. Since the fullback is aligned directly behind the ball, he is capable of blocking either flank with equal efficiency. This provides the offense with the capability of employing this type of passing action to either side of the offensive formation.

Unlike Play-Action Passes, the quarterback, using Sprint-Out Action, does not fake to a running back prior to attacking the flank. He simply sprints behind the fullback to the side of the pass.

With both Play-Action and Sprint-Out Passes, the quarterback has the option of running or passing the ball. If the fullback can hook the contain defender or kick him out enough to create a good inside alley, the Sprint-Out quarterback can read the defender responsible for the onside flat area and react to his movements. If the defender attacks the quarterback, the receiver in the flat is open. If the defender remains in the flat area, the quarterback can tuck the ball away and run for positive yardage.

THE SPRINT-OUT PASS FROM VARIOUS FORMATIONS

The Wing-T is basically a balanced offense with one halfback and one end to each side of the formation. This gives the offense the flexibility of having two receivers to both the onside and offside of the offensive formation.

This chapter deals with the Sprint-Out Pass from the basic balanced formation and does not get involved with any type of "Trips" formations.

The Sprint-Out Pass is normally executed to the side of the split end. The original alignment of this wide receiver horizontally stretches the defense and potentially creates soft spots in a zone defense. Sprinting to the split-end side may also get the defender, responsible for the offside deep outside one-third zone, too conscious of the onside and allow the offense to slip an offside receiver behind him for a quick six points. (Diagram 9-1)

DIAGRAM 9-1

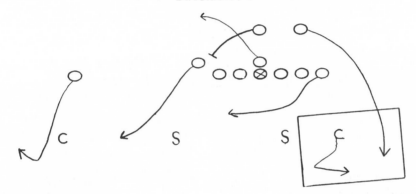

Using the Slant

On all plays, the two inside and the onside outside linebackers look at the formation to determine which receivers can possibly attack their areas of pass responsibility if the play is a pass. This practice is very important and greatly helps in underneath pass coverage.

The onside inside linebacker reads the area block of the onside guard. Since the guard does not come across the line of scrimmage, the linebacker reads pass. He sprints to his zone coverage area. As he drops, he checks number two. When number two releases vertically, the linebacker picks him up in the hook area. When number two releases horizontally, the linebacker looks to number one, normally a split end, running some type of inside route. (Diagrams 9-2, 9-3)

The offside inside linebacker reads the area block of the offside offensive guard. He checks his near back key and recognizes Sprint-Out Pass. He immediately drops into the hole and looks for an offside receiver running a drag pattern.

The nose tackle executes his slant and then rushes the passer.

When applying our basic Slant rules, the direction of the call can be toward the Sprint-Out Pass or away from it. The play of the ends, outside linebackers, and secondary is described under both circumstances in this chapter.

DIAGRAM 9-2

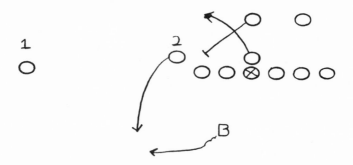

DIAGRAM 9-3

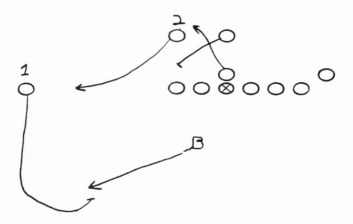

The following description applies when the defense is slanting in the same direction as the Sprint-Out Pass.

The onside end slants and is responsible for outside contain. He does not allow himself to be pinned or kicked out by the fullback. He fights through the block of the back and forces the quarterback to prematurely pull up.

The offside end, like the nose tackle, slants and, upon reaching his target point, rushes the passer.

The onside outside linebacker executes his slant and recognizes Sprint-Out Pass. He immediately sprints to the curl area to temporarily undercover an inside pattern by number one before picking up any receiver in the flat area. This drop buys time for the inside linebacker who is also sprinting to the curl area. This is particularly beneficial when number one is running a curl pattern. (Diagram 9-4)

The offside outside linebacker blitzes and rushes the passer. The offensive player responsible for picking up this defender is the offside offensive tackle. Since the tackle is originally covered by the offside end, he normally checks

DIAGRAM 9-4

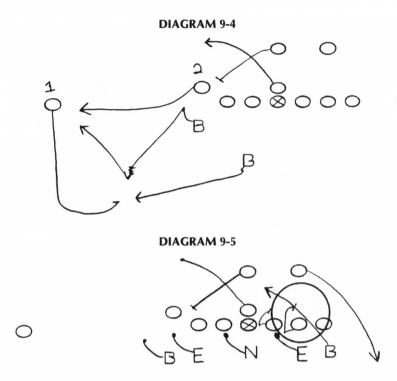

DIAGRAM 9-5

this player before going into his cup protection. This momentary delay can give the outside linebacker enough of an edge to beat this offensive lineman's block.

When the offside outside linebacker does beat the block of the offensive tackle, either the offside halfback picks him up or he has a clear path to the quarterback. (Diagram 9-5)

Some Wing-T teams are not very concerned about the offside outside linebacker. They feel, by his original alignment and the action of the quarterback, he will not get to the passer. However, when the onside end does a good job of containing the quarterback and forces him to prematurely pull up, the unblocked blitzer has a good chance of recording a sack or a hurry.

The secondary employs Roll coverage away from the Sprint-Out Pass. This puts the onside corner in the deep outside one-third zone. The offside corner, using Cup rotation, covers the offside flat area. The safeties cover the other two deep one-third zones. (Diagram 9-6)

When the Slant is called opposite the direction of the Sprint-Out Pass, the following reactions occur.

The onside end slants to the onside guard and is picked up by him. Upon recognition of the Sprint-Out Pass, he reacts to the quarterback and puts pressure on him. He may have to fight through the onside guard and tackle to get to the passer. The tackle, after stepping to the onside, has no defender to block and may react back to the inside to help the guard.

The offside end slants and becomes responsible for outside contain to the offside. After the threat of a Reverse is gone, he gets into the proper pursuit angle and attacks the quarterback.

The onside outside linebacker blitzes and jams the fullback. He forces the quarterback to pull up and puts immediate pressure on him. He is particularly careful not to allow the quarterback to get outside of him. He has contain responsibility.

The offside outside linebacker slants and covers the offside flat area. He employs his comeback technique since the quarterback is flowing away from him. He may end up helping the deep middle hook area.

The secondary employs Roll coverage in the direction of the Sprint-Out Pass. Both corners cover the deep outside one-third zones.

The onside safety, using Ivy rotation, goes through the curl area to cover any receiver in the flat zone. The offside safety covers the deep middle one-third zone. (Diagram 9-7)

DIAGRAM 9-6

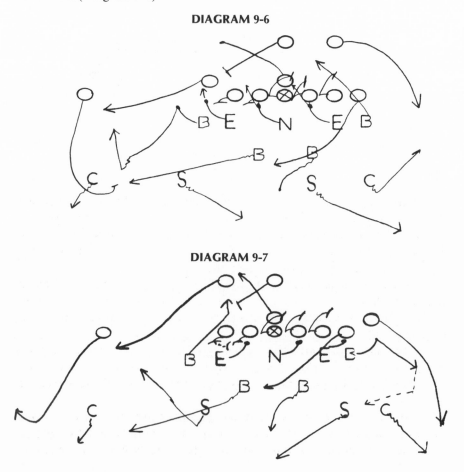

DIAGRAM 9-7

DIAGRAM 9-8

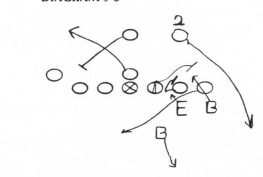

DIAGRAM 9-9

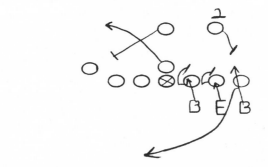

Using the Read Blitz

Versus a 3-4, some teams like to use a combination block on the offside. When the offside guard is left uncovered, he pulls to block the first defender outside the block of the offensive tackle. When offside number two sees no defender covering the guard and no inside blitz, he can release into the pattern and become the fourth receiver. (Diagram 9-8)

When the offside guard is covered, he stays in to block the defender aligned on him. Offside number two is forced to block the first defender to show outside the block of the offside tackle and cannot release for a pass. (Diagram 9-9)

The Read Blitz forces this second situation. However, when the guard steps up to block the Up linebacker, the linebacker drops into his zone coverage area. This leaves the guard with no defender to block and only three receivers in the pattern.

Both inside linebackers touch the guards on whom they are aligned. Since neither guard pulls, both guards execute their normal zone pass drops.

The nose tackle and both ends fight through the heads of the players on whom they originally align and put pressure on the quarterback. The onside end is responsible for outside contain.

The onside outside linebacker recklessly executes his blitz. He is not responsible for outside contain and can take some chances to make a Big Play.

The offside outside linebacker blitzes and pursues the quarterback. When the onside outside linebacker forces the quarterback to pull up, the offside outside linebacker may get to the passer.

The secondary, using He-Man coverage, employs man-to-man coverage on the receivers. Unless four receivers release, there is a free safety. (Diagram 9-10)

DIAGRAM 9-10

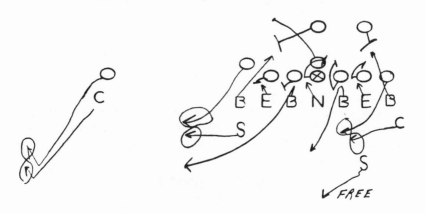

Chapter 10

Adjustments to Wing-T Variations

Along with the various pre-movement formations, pre-snap shifts, and the extensive uses of motion, the Wing-T Offense employs other significant formation variations. Two of the more common are the unbalanced line and the use of extended motion to create a "Trips" formation.

DEFENDING AGAINST THE UNBALANCED LINE

The "Tackle-Over" is the most commonly employed unbalanced line. This formation deploys an end to both sides of the ball. The tight end goes to the short side while the split end aligns on the unbalanced side. Both tackles align side by side on the unbalanced side. This "Over" tackle aligns where a tight end would be in a normal balanced formation. Most often, the halfbacks align as a slot to the unbalanced side and a setback to the short side. However, the placements of the halfbacks do vary. (Diagram 10-1)

DIAGRAM 10-1

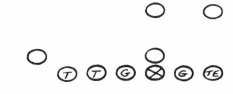

The unbalanced line is normally employed early in a game to determine what defensive adjustments will occur. The unbalanced line, like pre-snap shifts and the use of motion, is used to create a defensive weakness. Once a defensive weakness is recognized, the offense attacks that weakness. When no defensive weakness occurs, the offense normally abandons the use of the unbalanced line and attempts some other variation.

One important reason for all Wing-T variations is to cause numerous adjustments by a defensive team. It is hoped these many adjustments will cause defensive errors and give the offense a distinct advantage.

Even though we do make minor adjustments versus many Wing-T formation variations, we keep our basic defensive concepts intact. The Slant and Read Blitz function successfully against all Wing-T variations.

Using the Slant

We do not change our basic alignments versus an unbalanced line. We align as if the Over tackle is a tight end and the short-side tight end is a tackle. The outside linebacker to the short side aligns on an imaginary tight end.

Our secondary applies our basic rules with one minor exception. Versus a formation with only a tight end to one side and a wide receiver to the other, the safety to the tight-end side aligns over the guard or the third man in from the outside. The safety on the opposite side aligns three yards outside the tight-end position. Versus an unbalanced line, the safety to the tight-end side aligns over the center, the third man from the outside. The safety to the unbalanced side aligns three yards outside the normal tight-end position, which is occupied by the Over tackle. (Diagram 10-2)

Our basic Slant rules remain the same as do our Roll coverage rules. We slant to the side of the slot and our secondary employs Roll in the opposite direction. Versus the unbalanced formation, we execute the Slant to the unbalanced side and our secondary uses Roll coverage to the short side. The defense is still sound and only a minor secondary adjustment is required. (Diagram 10-3)

Using the Read Blitz

When Read Blitz is used, the only defensive adjustments (and they are very minor) are handled by the short-side corner and safety. Normally, the corner, playing the tight end man-to-man, aligns behind the outside linebacker. Versus the unbalanced line, the corner aligns behind the defensive end who is covering number one, the tight end. The safety, who is responsible for the setback who is number two, aligns over the short-side guard rather than the tackle. Aligning over the tackle would put the safety too close to the corner.

DIAGRAM 10-2

DIAGRAM 10-3

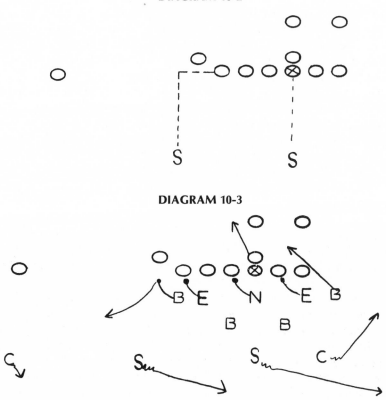

The alignment of the safety over the guard puts him inside the setback. This creates the definite possibility of a "Switch Call" between the safety and the corner. This possibility occurs versus a balanced formation but is much greater versus the unbalanced line.

DIAGRAM 10-4

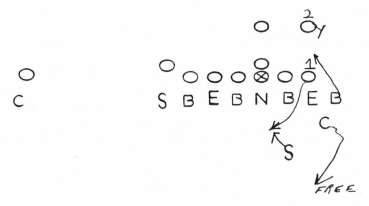

DIAGRAM 10-5

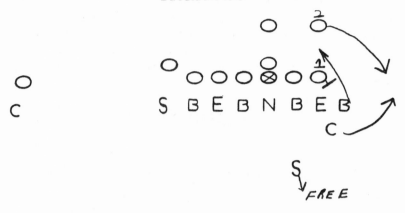

DIAGRAM 10-6

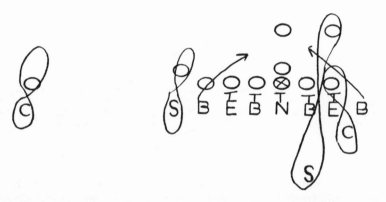

When number one releases inside, the corner calls Switch to the safety. The safety picks up number one and the corner picks up number two. When number two does not release, the corner becomes a free safety. (Diagram 10-4)

When number two releases outside, the safety calls "Switch," and the corner picks up number two. The safety takes number one man-to-man. When number one does not release, the safety becomes free. (Diagram 10-5)

The other defenders play the Read Blitz in the same manner versus the balanced and unbalanced lines. (Diagram 10-6)

DEFENDING AGAINST THE
TRIPS FORMATION

The Wing-T Offense can align in, shift to, or motion to several different Trips formations. The Trips can be to the side of the tight end or split end.

However, Trips most often occur to a slot flank. This is accomplished in two different ways. The setback employs extended motion and, on the snap of the ball, is between the slot and the split end. Another method is to align in a one-back set with the wing using extended motion to the slot flank. The defense handles both situations in much the same manner. (Diagrams 10-7, 10-8)

DIAGRAM 10-7

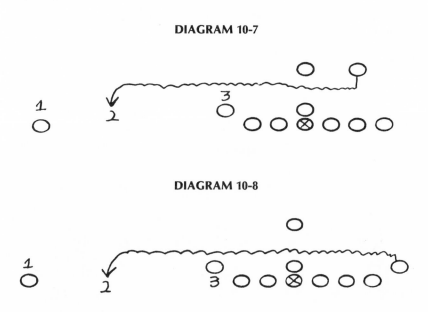

DIAGRAM 10-8

Like the unbalanced line, Trips are used early in a game to determine defensive adjustments and to exploit any defensive weaknesses created by these adjustments. If no offensive advantage is gained, Trips may be employed rarely during the contest.

Using the Slant

We do not change the alignments of our front seven defenders versus Trips. The linebackers, both inside and outside, the ends, and the nose tackle apply their basic alignment rules. The inside linebackers use the remaining one setback as their near back key.

The only adjustment to Trips is done by the safeties, and it is a minor adjustment. When the back in motion crosses the ball, the safety, who originally aligns on the tight-end side of the ball, moves to a position head-on the guard to the Trips side. The other safety widens with the motion man and keeps outside leverage on him until he crosses the split end. At this point, the corner widens with the motion man and the safety aligns on the outside shoulder of the split end. (Diagram 10-9)

DIAGRAM 10-9

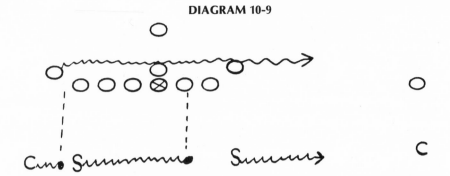

The Slant is executed toward the motion. The onside outside linebacker executes his Slant and, upon recognition of a drop-back pass or a passing action in his direction, drops into the near curl area before picking up any receiver in the near flat. The near curl and flat areas are located inside of number two.

Versus the Trips, the secondary employs Roll coverage in the same direction as the Slant. This provides two defenders to cover the curl-to-flat areas. Using Ivy rotation, the safety covers the far curl area before picking up any receiver in the far flat. The far curl and flat areas are located between number one and number two. (Diagram 10-10)

Since the Slant and Roll are in the same direction, the flat area away from the Trips is not covered. However, the corner to the side of the tight end has only one player who can immediately threaten his deep outside one-third zone. This player is the tight end. We feel the defender can cover this receiver as he slowly drops into his deep one-third zone. If no other receiver enters his zone, the corner can play the tight end man-to-man. (Diagram 10-11)

Using the Read Blitz

When using the Read Blitz, all defensive adjustments are handled by the secondary. When the wing goes in motion to the slot flank, there is only a tight end remaining. The corner takes him man-to-man. The safety moves with the motion man. When the motion man crosses the slot, the safety covering number two picks up the motion man, and the other safety picks up what has become number three. We bump our secondary defenders and do not stick with a receiver when he crosses another receiver. (Diagram 10-12)

Since there are four possible receivers on or near the line of scrimmage, there is no free safety. The secondary plays man-to-man coverage. The secondary defenders to the side of the trips must be ready to Switch when crossing patterns occur.

The front seven employ normal Read Blitz alignment and execute the defense. When all four receivers get into the pattern, we have one free front defender who cannot be blocked. A seven-on-six defensive advantage occurs.

DIAGRAM 10-10

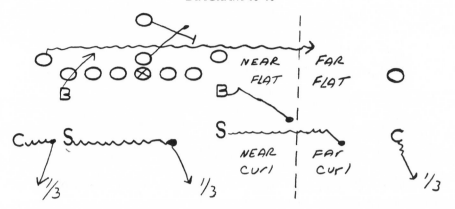

DIAGRAM 10-11

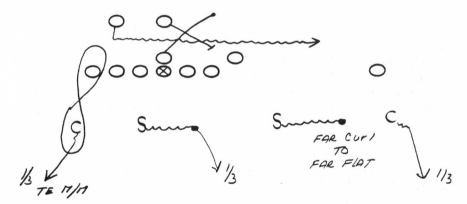

DIAGRAM 10-12

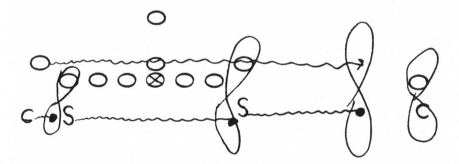